STRATEGIC PROGRAMME

COMMUNICATION

AND THE

NEW MEDIA DRIFT

STRATCOM EXPERTS
COMMUNICATION SOLUTIONS

ISAAC N. MBITHI

"Strategic Programme Communication and the New Media Drift"

By Isaac N. Mbithi
Copyright © 2015
by Author
All rights reserved.

ISBN: 978 1514186473

Table Content

List of Acronyms

1. CFS   Critical Success Factor

2. CVF   Competing Values Framework

3. CVFCC   Competing Values Framework for Corporate Communication

4. EOSL   External Operational Strategic Level

5. IOSL   Internal Operational Strategic Level

6. PCC   Programme Communication Culture

7. PfMP   Portfolio Management Professional

8. PgMP   Programme Management Professional

9. PMI   Project Management Institute

10. PMP   Project Management Professional

11. PMI-ACP   PMI Agile Certified Practitioner

12. SPC   Strategic Programme Communication

13. SRM   Stakeholders Relations Management

FOREWORD

The Forbes Insights 2010 Strategic Initiative Study reveals that 92% of CEOs, 92% of communicators and 88% of strategists hold the opinion that for their strategic programmes to succeed communication must be at the heart of all planning and execution processes, yet only 46% of all these categories admit having communication as an integral component of their strategies and execution processes. This clearly indicates that there is a big difference between what decision makers know as core to success of their strategic programmes and what actually happens. What goes wrong? A sizable number of managers who record some degree of success in programme management have a combination of skills, ranging from governance - establishing structural system, distribution of roles and responsibilities, supervision, Etc.; Management - planning, execution, evaluation of results etc., to systems and infrastructure development - establishment of physical, technological and social systems/ infrastructure. Yet, factors that influence performance of a manager stretch beyond individual's knowledge to how well the manager is able to use communication as a strategic instrument to mobilize both the internal and external stakeholders to support a common course of action. This is an additional set of skills often hard to come by. The situation is complicated by emergence of the New Media technology as an increasingly predominant channel of communication for both official and nonofficial purposes which too requires a new set of knowledge and skill.

It is within these circumstances that the author explores key concepts, parameters and a process through which programme managers can design and implement results based programme communication strategy to facilitate effective planning and execution of strategic initiatives. This book stands out among related materials in that it integrates theoretical interrogation of concepts with real life experience, enabling programme managers and persons in the related fields to think about programme communication in critical perspectives.

ACKNOWLEDGEMENTS

I am greatly indebted to Joseph Obwanda, a prolific writer and an outstanding motivational speaker who planted a seed of positivism in my heart and has since grown to generate this book.

I owe my wife Mercy Nikatsu, Dad Mr. Benjamin, Mum Alice, siblings Peter, Elijah, Esther and Dorcus, and the Itithi family many thanks for their support.

Nicholas Anyuor devoted his time in examining the manuscript content consistently. My gratitude is immeasurable.

Sincere gratitude to Prafulla Mishra (Phd) for spending valuable time within a tight schedule to technically review the manuscript. Your constructive feedback is much appreciated.

Finally, the primary debt remains to God the Most High for His never ceasing refinement, love and potency during the most trying spiritual and financial moments.

Isaac N. Mbithi
Nairobi, Kenya.

STRATEGIC PROGRAMME COMMUNICATION

INTRODUCTION:

The communication field has widely been researched and documented. Volumes of the documented content have themes ranging from basic communication skills such as writing effective emails, engaging in constructive dialogue, effective speech delivery etc., to technical communication skills useful in professions such as legal practice, medicine, engineering, technology and the media. Google search results as of 30th December 2014 show that 1.06 trillion (Google 2014) entries have been made, explaining general and technical communication in varied ways.

If you are a programme manager, you would probably have come across scores of these materials detailing diverse theories, strategies and norms that characterise organisational communication in general. While most of these theories, strategies and norms are as applicable in programme management as in any other organisational context, the role that effective communication plays in the success of any programme cannot be underrated. It is one of the Critical Success Factors (CFS) in programme management. CSF includes those processes or actions which must be executed for the programme to achieve its objectives. In fact a study conducted by Zayyna Shehu and Akintola Akintoye in 2009 to examine factors that are critical to the success of construction programmes in United Kingdom (UK) rated effective communication third (Shehu and Akintoye 2009) behind effective planning and establishment of programme priorities.

Being part of larger managerial team you are aware that success of the programme you are designing or currently managing is highly depended on how you win the support of the staff senior to you such as the directors, those directly and indirectly involved in the implementation of the programme under your supervision such as the coordinators or officers and the external stakeholders. The most important thing you need to have for success to manifest is the ability to tell others about the programme, convince them that you are pursuing a rewarding agenda and gain their support in performing functions necessary to make full implementation of the programme successful.

On the contrary, inability to effectively communicate and mobilise others to support your agenda can negatively affect the running of the programme. This may also diminish the possibility of realising the organisation's vision. You would obviously not want to see a new programme fail to take off because of lack of communication or avoidable communication blunders. You would also not want to see a programme you are managing crush midway simply because you can neither sustainably meet the information needs of your stakeholders nor solicit their commitment and support for the programme.

Gone are the days when employers used to employ secretaries for managers. The advent of computers and mobile telephones have predisposed most programme managers to a bigger responsibility not only in overseeing communication related programme functions, but also being the primary communicators for their programmes with both the internal and external stakeholders. Indeed, Mary Guffey and Dana Loewy 'Essentials of Business Communication' (Guffey and Loewy 2010) note that interpersonal (communication between individuals – in this case programme stakeholders) communication skills are more important today than in the past two decades and therefore it is not a requirement only for employees employed to facilitate organisational communication but an essential skills for all.

In a practical sense, as a programme manager, you will fall in one of the following THREE broad categories.

Category 1: Good in Programme Communication

- You have good skills in programme communication. You have a rich background in programme management. You probably secured a distinction in English course or any other official language of communication. Therefore, a combination of the managerial experience and language proficiency makes you a hot brand in the programme management field.

- You can communicate the programme objective and the strategy and convince others to support your course.
- You have excellent interpersonal skills and you can use them to mobilize teams to participate in a common course.
- Stakeholders find you approachable and have no qualms providing feedback on information you share with them.
- You can effectively use communication to motivate people to perform.
- You can use more than one channel to gather feedback from both internal and external stakeholders.
- You can use communication as a tool for empowerment of teams.
- You exhibit patience and resilience even when things appear to go haywire. Your emotions do not send the wrong signals to stakeholders.
- You know when to begin and end a discussion.
- You can anticipate how others will interpret your communication.

Category 2: Average in Programme Communication

- You have good programme experience and can articulate programme ideas in either written or speech form but sometimes your stakeholders find it difficult to understand what you mean. You often find yourself entwined in roundaboutness when developing or explaining a concept.
- You are struggling to ensure that the information you disseminate solicits the desired programmatic response. This may include timely feedback, timely submission of report, articulation of programme concepts as required, or at least acting as instructed.
- You can mobilize teams to deliver results but sometimes forget to timely share critical information.
- You cannot read all your mails in details. You sometimes realize when it is too late to correct the situation that you missed important details and therefore not likely to achieve the communication objectives.
- Teams often seek clarification but at least they find you approachable.

Category 3: Below Average in Programme Communication

- You have no specialised skills in programme communication despite a rich experience in programme management.

- You are not practically inclined or motivated to use strategic programmatic communication as an important instrument for success and therefore not aware that you are actually an impediment to effective programme delivery.

- You communicate without thinking through the idea and later regrets.

- You cannot clearly articulate what you intent to communicate.

- People hardly provide feedback on your requests.

- Stakeholders complain that you do not regard them as important.

- You react emotionally and sometimes behave erratically when something unpleasant is said about you.

- You cannot offer sufficient details to explain clearly an idea.

- You are not able to gather enough input/ideas from others before making decisions. Sometime you make a unilateral decision because you think consulting others is a waste of time.

If you are lucky to have good skills in programme communication (category 1), then you are an important assent to the programme. You have a greater capacity not only to effectively sell the programme strategy to the internal and external stakeholders but also get the stakeholders' commitment in the implementation of the programme. In some sectors, being an average person (category 2) in programme communication can be tolerated particularly if, and in rare circumstances, the sector specific technical skills are prioritised over communication skills. In other sectors it is not. If you are in category three you can still develop huge capacities in programme communication. All you need is to have a strategy: -grow your skills in Strategic Programme Communication (SPC) as this book proves. It is a process guide towards establishing results based programme communication.

It aims to achieve the following objectives:

- Examine some of the pointers of manifestation of effective communication within the programme stakeholders.

- Identify the key programme communication determinants

- Provide step by step guidance for developing results based programme communication strategy.

- Explore roll out approaches that promote achievement of the programme communication objective.

- Analyze programme communication opportunities within the new media technology spectrum.

So, what is SPC?

It is a combination of programme information exchange behaviours and processes meant to promote the achievement of the overall programme objective, and which form an integral component in the planning and execution of programmatic processes. SPC refocuses attention from a mare two way exchange of information by programme actors to a deliberate response by the programme manager and the team to the communication needs of other programme stakeholders and self. A well-executed SPC 'connects every member of the team a common set of strategies and actions' (Project Management Institute 2013). In this case, the programme manager and the team influences the manner in which other stakeholders communicate by taking lead in the development and roll out of a versatile programme communication strategy and ensuring that its components are well understood by stakeholders. The strategy guides the manager and the programme team in their engagement with the internal and external stakeholders.

There are two levels of SPC: (a) Internal and (b) External.

Internal SPC involves deliberate adoption of results oriented communication behaviours; proper internal networking, proactive dissemination of information, timely feedback and progressive improvement on best practices amongst internal programme stakeholders. SPC plays a functional role: - it helps in completion of tasks, creating and maintaining functional human relationships. Most often, programme communication is influenced by hierarchical structures interconnected by a network of channels along which information is transmitted to main units and sub-units. The internal communication networks can (collectively) be referred to as the communication climate. The climate is conducive when information flows freely within the team and across departments. On the other hand, the climate becomes non- conducive if information flow is blocked. Conducive climate is good because it is characterized by supportive, participatory, and trusting behaviours among the internal programme stakeholders, leading to higher productivity of team members and satisfaction, completion of tasks within the stipulated timeline and to the desired quality.

It is important to keep in mind that while internal communication may thrive, success of a programme is dependent on the support provided by and participation of external stakeholders who may include the target direct beneficiaries - for humanitarian and development programmes, customers for commercial programmes, the general public for advocacy or related programmes, the Government, none Government actors and even the international community. This diversity of external stakeholders also calls for strategic external communication, another key driver of effective achievement of the set goals.

External communication primarily involves proactive exchange of information with the external stakeholders through external communication networks. Establishing effective and sufficient external communication networks opens the programme to the good will of external stakeholders - thereby enhancing reliability and mutual support in execution of programme activities. Many approaches may be adopted to execute a results based programmed communication. However, every approach adopted should be a deliberate and a well-coordinated technical process characterized by a clear understanding of the prevailing situation, aspired situation and establishing mechanisms that guide the programme towards the attainment of the overall goal.

WHY EMBRACE STRATEGIC PROGRAMME COMMUNICATION?

Communication has long been treated as less an integral element of programmes management and more as an ad hoc element simply because it is a natural sociolinguistic aspect of all human beings. Yet it remains the pivot of effective programme management in the contemporary. In the opinion of Chuck Martin, 'the result of bad communication is a disconnection between strategy and execution" (Martin 2005). The Forbes Insights 2010 Strategic Initiative Study reveals that 92% of CEOs, 92% of communicators and 88% of strategists interviewed share the opinion that for their strategic initiatives to succeed (FTI Consulting 2010), communication lay at the heart of all planning and execution processes, yet only 46% of all these categories admitted having communication as an integral component of their strategies and execution processes at the time of the study.

Similar findings are documented in the Project Management Institute (PMI) 2013 Pulse, indicating that 55% of managers interviewed agree that effective communication to all stakeholders is a critical success factor in the completion of their projects. Unfortunately, many managers do not place importance on effectively communicating critical information especially when explaining the strategic importance of their initiatives and reporting of progress during and after implementation. The PMI's study further shows that of the 1 billion worth set of projects evaluated, USD 135 million worth projects in the Not-for-Profit and commercial sectors were high risk projects. Of these high risk projects 56% (USD 75 Million worth) were at risk due to ineffective communication (ibid). While the study shows that most managers were aware of the positive impact that effective communication can have on projects, it was not clear to most the impact of ineffective communication on project/programme outcome and the overall economic position of the organisations (Project Management Institute. 2013). PMI is a leading professional organisation for project, programme and portfolio managers and offers various credentials such as Project Management Professional (PMP), Programme Management Professional (PgMP), Portfolio Management

Professional (PfMP), PMI Agile Certified Practitioner (PMI-ACP) and others. PMI is the publisher for the Pulse of the Profession, an annual global research on topics related to project, programme, portfolio management and other management related topics (Project Management Institute 2014). These study statistics clearly reveal that much is always at stake when communication does not form part of the strategic initiatives in any programme management scenario. To mitigate the associated risks employing defined SPC should be an important dimension of all programmes. It is in practical sense the artery for coordination of activities and creating linkages that promote effective holistic planning and execution of programmatic initiatives. It is also being appreciated as a key process through which the financiers, consultants, managers, partners and contractors effectively exchange ideas/ information with the other stakeholders and includes responding to the specific communication needs of each stakeholder. These functionalities have been necessitated by the increased focus by stakeholders on accountability and the realisation that all inclusive stakeholder participation is essential in promoting sustainability and ownership of substantive deliverables.

Furthermore, the increasing use of the new media technology (communication through digital technology which includes but not limited to use of the internet, computer multimedia, digital publishing using CD-ROMs and DVDs and use of smart phones etc.) not only as a channel for communicating programmatic initiatives but as an interface for live saving information dissemination – in the case of humanitarian response, and redistribution of power of decision making (UN OCHA 2012), from the traditional wielders of information at the programme structure to other stakeholders illuminates on the benefits that programme management actors and other stakeholders are set to reap if strategy and execution are strategically linked through the digitally supported communication loop, among other channels of strategy communication.

(i) Internal Operational Strategic Level (IOSL)

Internally, strategic programme communication promotes systematic results driven programme communication to enhance implementation of programme activities; contribute to the realization of the programme goals, and establish a sustainable communication culture.

- Enhances implementation of programme activities – Programme communication acts as a vehicle for delivery of results. A well thought out communication can help in overcoming structural challenges by allowing managers to directly target communication to persons whose action is required while those affected by it are kept in copy for information only. This allows for timely action and feedback and mitigates the risk of unwarranted delay that characterise systems that require rigid adherence to protocol. On the contrary, lack of it becomes a bottleneck to effective functioning of various department and systems and hence a risk to the realisation of the programme goals.

- Contributes to short, medium and long-term programme goals - Having a well thought out communication strategy for the entire duration of the programme can help in consistent messaging to teams and external audience about results that are being achieved and lessons learnt.

- Establishes a sustainable programme culture - When programme communication best practices, tools and policies are accepted and adapted by the internal stakeholders as a way of doing things they form part of the Programme Communication Culture (PCC).

Scholars have explained communication culture in different ways:

- The established principles or value system that a group seeks to achieve (Geoff 2011).

- Policies and ideological values that influence a group's actions toward achieving the set goals (Ibid).

- The unwritten rules and regulations new personnel in an organization must adapt to work as a team with the other personnel or members of a group (Robert 2005).

The PCC informs the distinctive image of what internal stakeholders intend to achieve. It reflects practices that every member of the team should adopt. The culture is the long-term communication behaviour that is not affected by departure of some members of the programme team. New members are expected to gain awareness of the culture after which they become a part, adjust to it and effectively implement their roles. How well they know and adjust to the culture is determined by the information they receive during induction and after.

Two types of PCC exist; the strong culture and weak culture (Ibid). Strong culture is realized when the internal stakeholders consistently respond to a spur created through programme communication. The internal stakeholders find it easy and worth it to align to the communication value system of the programme articulated in the communication strategy. This makes operation of the programme cohesive; with minimal internal stakeholders communication disconnects or intrusion by new practices. The existing procedures are consistently executed. Strong PCC promotes order and harmony. This means that although internal stakeholders may hold differing opinions, their ideas may not derail the programmes best alternatives because dialogue and consensus would easily be attained. The internal stakeholders can easily ignore their independent ideas to support the ideas that are entrenched in the programme value system.

On the contrary is a weak communication culture. This culture is characterized by lack of order in the dissemination of information and reliance on rumour millers to access important programmatic information. Information is disseminated selectively and some team members who in real sense should be primary recipient of communication rely on proxies to gather important information. Providing feedback is not highly regarded and frequent conflicts characterize the internal working environment. This is dangerous for the programme because much time is spend on worrying about uncertainities, hinders teamwork, there is limited collective decision making, wrong decisions can bring down the programme.

(ii) External Operational Strategic Level (EOSL)

Programme communication is less useful if it is not properly implemented in coordination with external stakeholders. It requires integrating the substantive operational knowledge with effective mobilization skills to achieve the desired outcome, and is conducted with people outside the organization such as financiers, consultants, contractors, other partners, authorities, host communities, actors in the international community and/or beneficiaries.

If communication occurs in a multiple external stakeholders' context, efforts should be made to manage the communication in a framework that each stakeholder can closely associate with i.e. if a programme is being implemented by several implementing actors; each actor influences the operational success or failure of the other, and the degree of success in attaining the overall goal. Programme managers leading such a collection of stakeholders should therefore take stock of the existing frameworks, capacities of other stakeholders and develop a joint approach by engaging the stakeholders not only in consultations, but also in debates that seek to challenge some aspects of the preferred options in a communication framework before endorsement for implementation.

A good external programme communication Strategy should:

- Be inclusive

- Create proper space for public debates

- Disseminate dispassionate, accessible and credible information

- Create channels that enable the poor and marginalized to have their voices heard in the public arena or have their concerns addressed.

It is important to bear in mind that in the event that multiple stakeholders are implementing one big programme, they may use different approaches. As a result, the flow of information is influenced by the levels of inclusion of each stakeholder within and without the programme. When this situation manifest, anticipation of opportunities and challenges is essential in developing a mechanism that enables all parties to participate and own decisions made.

The following issues should be noted beforehand:

- In many devolved organizations, the operations between the Head Offices and the devolved levels may be disconnected: - the main office may not offer sufficient support to the local/ field offices/devolved structures. Similarly, the levels of devolution of decision making may vary across organisations which may affect efficiency of programme communication.

- Aspects of culture and political history should be put into consideration when developing a multi-sector-multi-stakeholder communication strategy. This is because some stakeholders have cultures that promote efficient performance of tasks, which creates impetus for timely responses and provision of feedback to communication disseminated to them, while others do not. Inefficient programme management structure may stall the progress of other stakeholders, affecting the entire intervention. In this case, decision making may require a systematic and long-term approach. If dealing with government authorities or bodies,the people's communication behaviour overtime forms the culture. This is often reflected in the governance and cultural practices which influence how the programme manager engages such stakeholders in programme communication. For example, some cultures require adherence to strict protocol when disseminating information to the community. This may include first getting the buy-in of the religious leaders or elders who would take up the responsibility of disseminating the information to the entire community. Others may provide opportunities to directly reach out to the target beneficiaries.

- Communication requires expertise input. In underdeveloped and developing countries where many humanitarian and development programmes are implemented, for example, there is often less focus on recruiting technical communication experts to support and coordinate strategic approaches to communication unless intended to carry out advocacy. This has led to minimal integration of the strategies developed by stakeholders into organizations' comprehensive communication framework. The private sector has on the contrary taken up abitious initiatives to promote strategic communication and some departments such as public relations or internal/external communication have been established.

- Stakeholders may be diverse. The need for inclusive planning may bring together people who have proper understanding of communication strategy development and execution and others who lack the capacity to execute the strategy. In this situation, proper mechanisms should be put in place to ensure that sending and receiving of messages are not affected by capacity differences.

- Relevance of the communication channel. In programme communication, the channel should be that which many of the stakeholders are familiar with; have ownership of; and is in agreement with social values within dynamic cultural, social, and political spectra. Differences in media preference may hinder information reception and dissemination. They may also render message delivery ineffective when evaluated besides the goals and objectives of the initiatives. This situation is common where new media rather than the traditional media (traditional media includes the broadcast and cable television, radio, movie, newspapers, magazines, books and other printed publications) is used as a mode of information exchange and dialogue. For example, the youth may be highly engaged in communication through new media platforms such as the Facebook, Twitter, Skype, MySpace or Flicker while programme managers and organizational leaders may put emphasis on use of magazines or radio programmes, which may not be popular among the youth (if the programme has the youth as the main beneficiaries). The preference difference presents disconnect in flow and delivery of information. In addition, some of the old media are one way: - they do not provide room for real-time feedback from the recipients. The area of coverage is also limited. This hinders communication between the stakeholders.

WHAT CONSTITUTES RESULTS BASED PROGRAMME COMMUNICATION?

A results based programme communication is characterized by the manifestation of Efficiency, Inclusiveness, Relevance and Predictability.

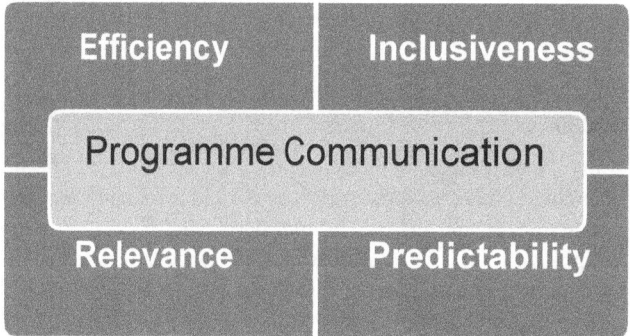

a. Efficiency

The results of a communication process should be determined beforehand. The result should be based on the needs of the stakeholders not in opposition. This can be referred to as the target situation. Actions meant to achieve the outcome should be well articulated and every aspect of the communication package, including modes, themes and targets should be well thought of to ensure that the communication prompts the intended response by the stakeholder.

The right message should reach the right audience at the right time and place. In some circumstances the situation changes, rendering the initial communication less useful. This calls for evolving response through real-time updates to ensure that the communication is relevant to the stakeholders and reflects the changing situation and audience.

The effectiveness of a message is determined by the succinctness of concepts articulated. Messages should be clear and to the point. Ambiguity, repetition and roundaboutness may hinder interpretation of the main idea. For instance, an idea may be expressed in nine sentences of two paragraphs whereas such an idea can be put across in a single clause. SPC requires avoiding unnecessary information and details that might put off the recipients.

In changing and adversarial situations, the speed of communication is essential because it determines the ability of the stakeholders to act on the communication. Due to possible differences in the audience, a programme manager should exercise high levels of flexibility to effectively address specific issues affecting specific audiences. There exists inherent risk in all communication. Therefore, sharing only what is needed for specific stakeholders ensures that sensitive information does not go to those not intended.

b. Inclusiveness

Programme communication should enhance cohesiveness of both the internal and stakeholders. This is an indicator of success and it is highly depended on the manifestation of inter-personal or inter-departmental communication. It is also important to bear in mind that inter-personal or inter-departmental communication promotes cohesion if all the parties involved receive the message without distortion(Department of Defence,United States of America, 2008). All the actions, words and images should be done with a clear intent and guidance to avoid misinterpretation, subordination, intimidation, or misinformation.

The pyramid below illustrates the buildup process for setting the programme communication objectives. The foundation should be the value system of the masses which include the social, political and cultural contexts. This should be followed by a critical analysis of the value system of the main stakeholders. All internal stakeholders are considered main as what they communicate and how they do it in the work environment and sometimes outside the work environment influence the degree of success in the programme implementation. Main external stakeholders include those whose communication or acts of information dissemination directly impacts on the programme implementation. They include external financiers, consultants, contractors, external beneficiaries of the programme, opinion leaders etc.

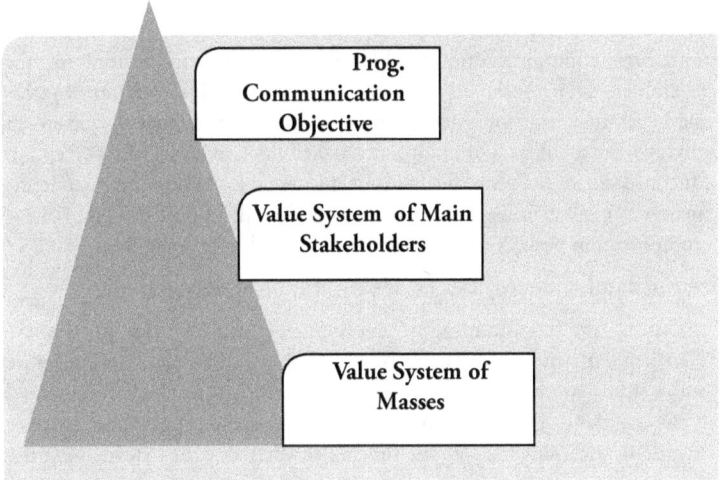

In each communication oriented action, the following should be put into consideration:

- The desired outcome should be aligned with the major lines of operation of each stakeholder.

- Comparison and realignment should be done to create a common focus in a manner that does not contradict any stakeholders' operation policy guidelines.

- The actions and ideas of the stakeholders should be linked to form the strategic plan.

Successful programme communication among multiple stakeholders is based on leveraged leadership:-where every participant is considered equally important. An established good relationship helps the stakeholder to proactively share new information or provide actionable feedback. Therefore, a programme manager should always plans for a time to strengthen relationships with stakeholders through either structured or unstructured dialogue and in line with the stakeholders' sociocultural discourse. This promotes trust among them.

c. Relevance

Programme communication should meet the information needs of the stakeholder. It involves dissemination of credible information. In this regard, all images, words and actions must be coordinated within an individual stakeholder and among the stakeholders without the perception of inconsistencies between the words or images created and the actual deeds. Furthermore, all actions, images and words should support the programme communication policy's overarching objective and long-term plans.

The communication may lack credibility because of several reasons:

- During the communication development process, the programme manager may not be well conversant with the subject matter and therefore the information transmitted may either misrepresent facts or mislead the recipient. This situation can be avoided if the programme manager gathers sufficient facts about the subject matter before developing the message.

- The message may be out of date. Other events may have rendered the applicability of the concepts articulated in the message irrelevant. To avert this situation, the programme manager should be well versed with the changes in the context to encode relevant messages.

Communication theorists have endeavoured to extrapolate how communication happens –the resulting processes will be discussed in details in a later section of this material. Some have advanced arguments that the meaning lies in the message; that the correct meaning is known by the sender who also constructs the message and may be distorted by the channel during transmission; that the meaning is as interpreted by the receiver and still others argue that the environment influences the meaning of meaning.

All these schools of thought present key communication attribute:- message processing and feedback, direct experience of a phenomenon, human interaction, interpretation of expressions, influence of ideas, (re)creation of a system/order, reflection and general understanding of artistic discourse.

These can be summarized as; for a message to be relevant, stakeholders have to have the ability to process the message and provide feedback, share experience of the other and adjust the feedback accordingly, interact as human beings, and influence each other in a system or social order - as in the case of a programme.

Strategic communication plans should be all-encompassing. Every action, word or image should send a message. It is important to bear in mind that all stakeholders communicate either consciously or subconsciously and all aspects of communication can have an impact on the overall plan. For instance, the information may be transmitted to unintended audiences (which in some cases is an unavoidable situation) or properly coordinated to make the desired impact. When the information is relayed to unintended audiences, it may either be irrelevant or expose the programme to a risk. Caution should therefore be taken to ensure that information dissemination is matched with the information needs of the programme stakeholders.

Relevance is sustained by embracing a proactive approach to communication; SPC should be an ongoing process involving research, analysis, planning, execution, evaluation and receiving of feedback, as shown in the flow chart below.

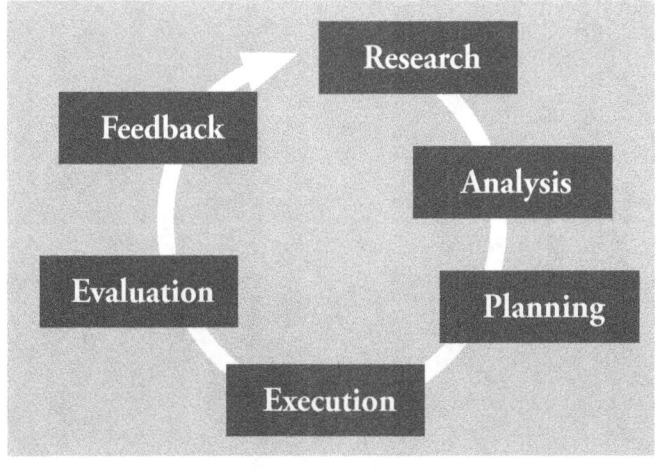

Therefore, success of the communication process is determined by the degree of adherence to due diligence and continual investigation of the process, collection of feedback and review of the strategy to improve on the effectiveness/impact. Continuous review ensures that the plan supports the programme objective.

4. Predictability

Strategic programme communication requires putting in place and adherence to some basic guidelines for information dissemination. For example, it should detail what information should be disseminated to specified stakeholders within a laid down periodicity. This enables stakeholders to plan for corresponding communications in time and minimizes multiple requests for information or clarification. This also enables the programme manager to respond to the issues arising from the information disseminated in a conclusive manner, as they can compare feedback and combine responses that are related or share a more elaborate feedback to address multiple concerns of different persons. In some instances, setting specific dates for receiving feedback from the stakeholders enables the managers to plan in a manner that allows for advancing of other agenda in task lists. Some of the examples of periodical communications include programme reports, periodic update, dashboard reports etc.

KEY MILESTONES TOWARDS RESULTS-BASED PROGRAMME COMMUNICATION

R esults based programme communication involves three main steps;

a. Identifying context specific programme communication determinants.

b. Developing actionable strategy.

c. The rolling out the programme communication strategy.

A). IDENTIFYING CONTEXT SPECIFIC PROGRAMME COMMUNICATION DETERMINANTS

Communication theorists have laboured to explain the drivers of effective communication. Years of research and analysis have culminated in a number of theoretical arguments that shade some light on some of the determinants of effective programme communication when analysed in view of most common programme communication behaviours.

This section examines some of the theories advanced in the communication field in order to provide a platform for deciphering various determinants of effective programme communication. For clarity, the determinants will be contextually analysed and a summary of possible corrective actions will be detailed. These determinants and corresponding measures form points of reference when carrying out the actual development of programme communication strategy. Reference to the communication theories will provide the following benefits;

- They will help make use of theoretical perspectives of communication processes while providing leeway for exploring vantage points that explain programme communication determinants.

- Theories will provide a platform for clarifying complexity of communication processes. They will help make clearer the structure of a complex communication processes by reducing the subtle concepts to simpler and understandable terms and link them to the programme communication process.

- Theories will help in interrogating communication processes beyond the common codes to a real situation simulated perspective. In doing this they will offer new insights into concepts, which will enable improvement of programme communication in a manner that succinctly meets the programme communication objective.

It is however not within the scope of this book to create new theories of communication or provide an in-depth critique of the existing theories. In view of the operational context of most stakeholders involved in programme communication, emphasis is laid on the elements of communication which have the biggest impact in programme communication.

It is also important to note that when communication is interrogated within a theoretical framework, models are developed - a simulation of the communication process. Therefore, juxtaposed with the theoretical interrogation, reference will be made to the in-vogue models; this is not intended to showcase them as the preferred theories of communication (whether classical or modern) but as a basis for carrying out a comparative analysis of some of the basic elements that cut across most of the theories and determine in one way or another effectiveness of programme communication. In instances in which a determinant manifests in more than one theory, only the unique elements will be discussed in the proceeding theories.

The main theories of reference include: The Mediation by Signs (Semiotics), Schramm, Mehrabian (also known as 3Vs model) theories.

A.1 THE MEDIATION BY SIGNS (SEMIOTICS)

The model was advanced by Sociolinguist Ferdinand de Saussure, (1857–1913). Although commonly known as a linguistic theory of production and interpretation of meaning, its focus on interpersonal communicate makes it one of the oldest theories of communication often ignored when theorizing communication. Its relevance in the context of programme communication is mainly derived from the fact that programmes are implemented in multi-stakeholders contexts, and run by people with diverse cultural and linguistic backgrounds, conditions that influence the way they communicate with the programme internal and external stakeholders.

The analysis of this model provides six determinants of effective programme communication: Primarily, communication involves two entities; the sender and receiver. It is influenced by the code, context, message and contact (Saussure 1983).

Context

Message

Sender (Encodes signs).......... Receiver ....(Decodes/interpretes meaning)

Contact

Code

De Saussure's mediation by signs argument can be simulated in programme communication process as follows; the Programme Manager (Sender) generates the message (encodes signs) influenced by the system of rules that define his/her understanding of subject matter and by the communication environment (context) and transmits it through a medium (Contact) such as e-mail, letter, internet, one on one meeting etc. to the stakeholders (receivers). The stakeholders (receivers) interpret (decode) to decipher the intended communication by the programme manager. The meaning is determined by a combination of the receivers system of rules which may be significantly different from the programme manager's codes.

The following is the extrapolation of the different communication determinants:

Code: De Saussure argues that signs have a role in human social life. The nature of signs influences the rules that govern them with a clearly defined place in human knowledge. These rules are called the codes and they link signs to meaning. For example in English language the codes are inform of grammar or syntax. Similarly, people understand and organize phenomenon differently in the mind. The way they understand influences how they transmit their understanding to other people.

What to do:

- Communicate using language commonly known and used by the stakeholders.

- Remember that an object may have different meaning in stakeholders community than that you know, particularly if you are from a different speech community.

- Use simple and direct language: - avoid ambiguity/vagueness as much as possible, be precise and focus on the main points.

- Anticipate the possible interpretation by the stakeholders and adjust the communication to ensure that only the intended message is transmitted.

Contact: This is the chosen medium of transmission. It is important to note that the choice of the medium is determined after assessing the appropriateness of each option to the stakeholders. This is because effectiveness in programme communication is promoted when the message is transmitted through the most suitable medium for the selected audience/stakeholders.

What to do:

- Use words that are least misinterpreted by the stakeholders.

- Consult with stakeholders when using symbols such as logos, drawing, human or animal images etc.

- Consider the influence of the culture in interpreting meaning of signs and symbols.

Message: This is the communication. How clear the message is framed determines how correct it is interpreted. Long unclear sentences may result to ambiguity, misinform the recipients of the communication, delay the processing of feedback, cause conflict among the stakeholders and contribute to missing out on important deadlines.

The following conversation was extracted from an email thread between a programme manager and a programme coordinator during a content review exercise;

Programme Manager: Please provide further breakdown of the number of girls and boys who occupied the new and existing classrooms. The disaggregation of the data is necessary for measurement of the project performance.

Project Manager: 3,322 (1,434 girls and 1,888 boys) learners occupied the new and existing classrooms.

First interpretation: The programme manager was requesting for data of learners, disaggregation by gender, who occupied both the new and existing classrooms.

Second Interpretation: The programme manager was requesting for four levels of data disaggregation; girls who occupied the new and those who occupied the old classrooms on one hand and boys who occupied the new and those who occupied the old classrooms on the other.

The programme coordinator deciphered the first interpretation and provided only two levels of disaggregation while in actual sense the programme manager required the four categories of data. This situation meant that the programme manager needed more time to provide the four types of data, which may cause missing out on important deadlines.

This communication would be made more comprehensible by breaking down the communication in a simple tabular format as illustrated below;

Classrooms/Learners	Boys	Girls	Total
Learners who occupied the new classrooms	xx	xx	xxxx
Learners who occupied the old classrooms	xx	xx	xxxx
Total	xxxx	xxxx	xxxxxxxx

Furthermore, interpretation of a message can go beyond the surface meaning of the codes to include; the mood of the sender, the attitude towards the receiver, the action articulated in the message and whether a feedback is needed or not. Clear and articulate message induces the right interpretation, the right action and feedback. Obscure communication brings in confusion and may lead to mis-action which may be detrimental to the programme as a whole.

What to do:

- Focus on the quality. Develop precise and orderly message. If written text, avoid long sentences which may be difficult to understand.
- If using video/PowerPoint presentation, ensure the message stands out rather than animation.
- Make the communication relevant.
- Communicate in sufficient quantity: - not more or less than meets the stakeholders information needs.

Context: The message is sent within a context/communication environment. For instance, if a message is send while in a refugee camp from an agency, the context is the composition of all communities represented both within the refugee community, the host community and agency workers. The context influences the nature of the message because it requires the sender to understand the system of signs and meanings assigned to the signs by the communities, and use them appropriately to transmit the desired message. Often, when programme managers work in communities outside their native community such as in international humanitarian agencies, they work in a culture different from the culture that prearranged meaning to signs as they grew up. The same signs may be found in the new environment. It is important to note that although the signs may be similar, the meaning may be different.

Context is an important determinant in that it covers understanding of the physical, cultural, linguistic, psychosocial and psychological state of reference of the stakeholders and self:- The person conceiving and articulating the message is influenced by his/her physical, social, cultural or linguistic orientation. These may include the situation they are in, what they know about the subject matter, the anticipated impact of the message, attitude towards the recipient etc.). Similarly, receivers of the communication interpret the meaning influenced by their physical, psychological, social, cultural or linguistic orientation.

What to do:

- Use words that are least likely to be misinterpreted by the stakeholders.
- Consult with stakeholders when using symbols such as logos, drawing, human or animal images etc.
- Consider the influence of the culture in interpreting meaning.

Sender: The Manager is responsible for developing the programme communication, ensuring that whatever is communicated is relevant, not outdated and meets the information needs of the receiving stakeholder (s).

What to do:

- Remember that you may not always properly communicate what you intend. Ultimately what you transmit matters.
- Invest time and resource wise in preparing communication: Spend some time gathering facts, important statistics and figures and ensuring that they are correct, seeking clarification for colleagues or verifying if in doubt about some of the issues to be communicated.

Receivers: The receivers include both internal and external stakeholders. The programme manager should anticipate each stakeholder's information needs and generate a communication that meet the stakeholders needs in terms of the type and clarity of the communication. The knowledge of stakeholders extends to signs which have direct meaning within the linguistic discourse and which can be interpreted to generate indirect meaning. In light of this, De Saussure highlights two levels of meaning interpretation: - denotative and connotative, both of which a programme manager should be conscious of to ensure that the message generated and transmitted conveys the intended communication.

Case Illustration 2: Semiotics case analysis

I. A proverb in the Somali community states that, 'hal far ah fool madaqdo'. The denotative meaning is that one finger cannot wash the whole face. However, the meaning intended to be conveyed is that one person cannot complete a daunting task/work alone. This is a call for partnership and collaboration. Use of the stakeholders' coding system while communicating to them brings the message closer to the intuitive order of their minds.

II. In the Somali community, a click of the tongue means acceptance. In the Kamba community in Kenya and Tanzania, the same sound is used to express annoyance.

Denotative meaning is the simple interpretation assigned by a community to a sign, and can easily be understood by members of the community who understand the general language of the people. Conversely, connotative interpretation goes beyond the surface meaning. It entails adding new shades of values and culture to understand signs or expressions made without the focus on the meaning commonly known by the people. These differences in interpretation may cause misunderstanding if the meaning is not derived from the context and ultimately hinder the communication processes.

What to Do

- The message to stakeholders should be transmitted in a simple and clear form, keeping in mind the invisible possible influence of the context and to avoid ambiguity while generating the message.
- It is advisable to develop knowledge of the areas of semantic/meaning differentiation. Strategic programme communication involves identification of the meaning systems of a stakeholder and flexibly addressing the challenges that hinder understanding of the message conveyed.

A.2 Schramm Theory of Communication

The Schramm theory of communication deviates from the De Saussure's Mediation by Signs theory by putting more emphasis on interactivity of communication (circularity of communication), effects of noise in the transmission of the communication and influence of field of experience. The in-vogue model contains: source/encoder, message, channel, decoder, and receiver. In addition to these determinants the model incorporates feedback, noise and field experience, making it a better reflection of programme communication process.

Fig: Schramm Communication Model of 1957.

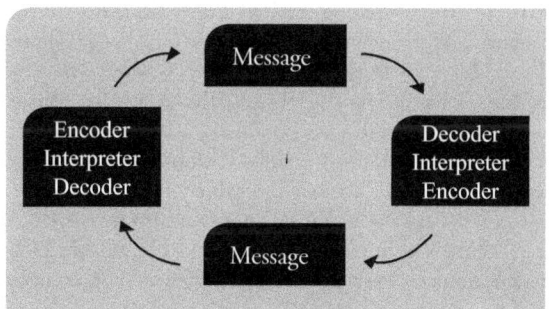

The encoder is the person who conceives the idea and contextualizes it. According to Schramm, the encoder is the person who takes the field experience (the state of mind or psychological frame of reference) and encodes/prepares it (converting the experience into transmittable forms such as text, sound or picture) for transmission. The construct is transmitted inform of a message to the intended stakeholder referred to as the interpreter/decoder who after interpreting the message prepares/encodes a feedback and sends back to the encoder and the process continues in a circular process.

Feedback: In order for interpreting stakeholder to give the right feedback, the right message must be decoded/ interpreted. One may ask; do all communications require feedback? Some people may think that some communications are shared for information only. However, acknowledgement of receipt of the communication is very important. It shows that the communication, if it requires action by the receiving stakeholder, is being acted upon. Feedback is needed for both interactional and transactional communication. It builds relationships, strengthens teamwork, and helps in resolving either manifested or anticipated conflict. It is useful in gauging understanding and how well the message has been received and helps in either seeking or providing clarification among other functionalities. Responsiveness in provision of feedback promotes effective programme communication. Therefore, it is a central determinant of effectiveness of programme communication.

Field Of Experience: The great philosopher Immanuel Kant in his critique of pure reason argues that 'There can be no doubt that all our knowledge begins with experience... and the reason is by nature architectonic (1781-1789) (Kant 1965). Two phrases stand out in this critique; first that knowledge begins with experience and that this knowledge is architectonic:- characterized by a systematic unity of knowledge of general objects, the rationalization of different objects and knowledge of them in a manner that promotes order and harmony in relation to the world as a whole. Communication per se is a process of dissemination of this knowledge gained from experience. Evidently, there is a direct link between acquiring knowledge from experience and sharing the same. The link is in the existence of a systematic unity, which in programme communication context manifests when the stakeholders have a shared knowledge of the subject matter and/or associated phenomenon.

This opinion is shared in the above model; Schramm includes influence of the field of experience in encoding and decoding the message and relates to communication behaviours that meet the communication needs of all stakeholders. For example, if a programme manager request for a programme brief from the programme officer, both have an overlap in their fields of experience and therefore the feedback is likely to be relevant or satisfactory. This is not so if a monitoring and evaluation manager requests for data validation information from a project officer who does not have a monitoring and evaluation background. Both have either limited overlap in their fields of experience and therefore there is a likelihood of a communication breakdown between them. Furthermore, this situation may create a working environment lacking supporting behaviours.

Noise: Schramm looks at noise not as a promoting determinant of communication but as a hindrance. It can be categorized into four; the physical noise (the noise generated within the environment which interferes with hearing ability of the receiver), Psychological (preconceived notions by the receiver which hinders correct interpretation of the message), semantic (improper choice of words or differences in literacy levels between the communication actors) and physiological (lack of/diminished sense of hearing). As a Programme Manager it is important to be aware of these hindrances in order to put in place corrective measures. Effective programme communication requires avoidance of noisy working environment, articulateness, attentiveness, use of simple words and positive attitude.

In practical sense, stakeholders may be influenced in the communication by one or all of the determinants derived from this model, but with varied levels of intensity.

Consider the following dialogical case illustration of programme communication.

Ngiliki is a programme manager for the Child in Emergency (CiE) programme run by Polipo Foundation. The programme has four components/projects; education, provision of emergency shelter, protection and emergency food security, each component implemented by a project manager.

Ngiliki supervises the four project managers: Joseph, Jong, Amina and Kagawa. These projects are implemented in four different locations while Ngiliki base station is the Polipo Foundation's head office. Ngiliki writes a mail to the Projects Managers reminding them of an upcoming end of programme report, and requesting them to submit their projects inputs in two weeks time for consolidation into a final report.

'Dear All,
This email serves as a reminder that the end of programme report is due in two weeks time. Attached please find the reporting templates. Do not hesitate to contact me in case any section of the templates is not clear.

Two days before the deadline, Ngiliki does not receive any feedback and therefore shares a second reminder!

Ngiliki: Hi colleagues, hope you still remember that the report is due in two days!

Jong: Hi Ngiliki, Sorry, I forgot to write back earlier; kindly share the reporting template.

Ngiliki: (Annoyed...bangs the table and...) Look at this fool, two weeks now! Ngiliki refers to the first reminder e-mail shared with the team and confirms that the template was actually attached. 'wwwfff', Ngiliki retorts.

You see!!! The templates are already attached in the email I shared earlier. I do not understand what some people see when they click their inbox....the communication is also clear. They should have asked for clarification immediately!

The following morning, Joseph writes to Ngiliki.

Joseph: 'Ngiliki ... kindly accept my apology, I have been in a stakeholders training workshop for a week. I have also been busy coordinating emergency response meetings. My assistant is on annual leave and I am the only one who can handle this. Furthermore, I have not received the evaluation report from the monitoring and evaluation officer. Immediately I receive this, I shall share with you the report.

Ngiliki: okay Joseph, please suggest the most appropriate date that you would be able to share the report with me!

Joseph: I am not sure; it depends on how fast I get the project monitoring and evaluation report.

Ngiliki: Can I suggest in three days time, and then you ensure that the monitoring report is received on time... and that all performance indicators are responded to?

Amina: Good evening Ngikili, attached is the project report. Please let me know if you need additional details.

Kagawa: Good morning Ngiliki, attached is the draft report. It wasn't clear to me what to include and what to omit. I have therefore provided as much information as possible.

Ngiliki: Dear Amina, Kagawa. Thanks both for the reports. The information provided provides sufficient input into the final report for your sectors.

Joseph: (A day after the due date) Hello Ngiliki, attached is the project report but does not have the monitoring details. I will share these later.

Jong: (Two days past the due date) Hello Ngiliki, attached please find the shelter report.

Ngiliki: (reads through the shelter report and realizes that Jong never followed the instructions. Most of the sections are blank and much of the needed data is missing). Too bad! Ngiliki murmurs, picks her telephone and calls Jong:

Ngiliki: Hello Jong, I have received the report but it is all useless. You have not measured the outcome. You never followed instructions both in the template and in my e-mail communication.

Jong: Sorry for that. I am an engineer, ask me what I have constructed not the impact.

(Ngiliki logs off the computer knowing well that the donor report would not only be submitted late but also that documentation of the impact would be compromised).

The above dialogical case is a simulation of common occurrences in programme communication. While in-depth semantic analysis (connotative level analysis) of the text may bring forth a multiplicity of interpretations, a surface meaning level of interpretation of at least three determinants may help in highlighting possible corrective measures to ensure results based programme communication manifests.

(i). The Feedback determinant: While Ngiliki's expectation is that the project managers understood the email communication and therefore did not have a reason to write back, it appears that Joseph and Jong did not either read the instructions until the second reminder was send or didn't understand but refrained from requesting for clarification.

(ii). Noise: There is a clear indication of manifestation of noise as a deterrent of effective communication:

- *Psychological:* The relationship between Ngiliki and the project managers is evidently distant. Ngiliki assumed that their only point of concordance was through the email, yet that did not address other context influenced challenges that the project managers experienced. That too does not appear to be Ngiliki's concern, but the report. It is important to note that the pure act of sending an email is not an evidence of effective communication. Programme communication requires proactive follow up actions such as Skype chats or telephone call as the situation may allow, which must be characterized by positive attitude and supportive behaviors. Ngiliki's reaction on the shortcomings of the project managers further portrays an impatient, non-supportive and a nagging character: - Ngiliki is the boss, the project managers are the servants. Furthermore, there might have been past confrontations/disputes and subsequent growth of negative attitude which make the managers less responsive to Ngiliki's request.

- *Semantic:* The email might have been elusive. It appears that Jong might have read the email, but didn't decipher the communication as intended: (a) the communication did not have specified the timelines within which the request for further clarification was required and therefore despite Ngiliki's furry Jong provided feedback (b) The project managers appear to have interpreted the communication differently. Amina and

Kagawa submitted their reports within the stipulated timeline. Jong and Joseph did not. Joseph only gives excuses once the second reminder is received while Jong realizes that he did not have the right templates. This situation implies that both never worked on the report for the period before the second reminder and therefore they would either not meet the deadline, or they would not provide all what is needed in quantity and quality. This situation requires proactive approach from both sides. The programme manager should ensure that the communication is precise and void of information overload. If possible, the main points should be either numbered or in bullet points. Second, the programme manager should have begun tracking the progress in the development of the report immediately the first reminder was send with two main objectives: to ensure that the managers read and understood the content and to identify if there was any additional support needed to complete the report.

(iii) Variance in the fields of experience: The programme manager oversees four different technical sectors. Chances are that Ngiliki does not have technical competence in one or more of the sectors. On the other hand, only two project managers – Amina and Kagawa have been able to submit their inputs on time with the required information. Jong and Joseph do not. Jong is not bothered by the measurement of impact indicators because he is an engineer and therefore he has no background experience in either M&E or reporting impact of projects. Joseph too does not provide the impact details because he is possibly a sector specific technical person and has to rely on the monitoring and evaluation department for this information.

However, it appears he was not able to coordinate the monitoring and evaluation exercise properly and therefore this information is evidently missing by the time of writing the report. This is a failure on his part because he never anticipated the donor communication needs during the implementation of the project.

The table below is a summary of the derived determinant, simulated challenges and possible measures that could ensure effective programme communication.

No.	Determinant	Simulated Challenges	Possible Solutions
7	Feedback	• Late request for templates. • Incomplete reports • Late submission of reports.	• Provide prompt/timely feedback. • Ensure that the feedback sufficiently meets the information needs of the stakeholders. • Convey feedback in a clear to understand format. • Request for or proactively seek feedback if necessary.
8	Field of Experience	• Inability to provide all the required information. • Diverse fields of experience/ competencies.	• Determine if the recipient of your communication has the capacity to act upon it. • Evaluate the capacity gaps by identifying managers/ stakeholders who need additional support. • Provide timely support either directly or by mobilising technical resources such as contracting a consultant.
9	Noise	• Psychological noise- negative attitude, discordance among the actors. • Semantic- unclear communication. • Physiological: inability of the project managers to read exhaustively the communication.	• Psychological - Take consideration that psychological noise is inevitable and adopt positive attitude while communicating with stakeholders. • Semantic – be precise and use easy to understand words or symbols. • Physiological- Perceive the limitations of the receiving stakeholder and choose a medium that meets their needs or provide the necessary support mechanism. For example, frequent reminders.

A.3 MEHRABIAN THEORY

This theory was advanced by Albert Mehrabian in 1981 during his study on the relative importance of verbal and non-verbal messages. The study unveiled the 7%-38%-55% message delivery tenet. Basically, efficacy of communication is influenced by the degree at which the communicator uses the 3Vs, namely: verbal, vocal and visual. Verbal communication conveys only 7% of the meaning; vocal conveys 38% while 55% of the message is communicated visually.

3 VS ROLE IN MESSAGE DELIVERY

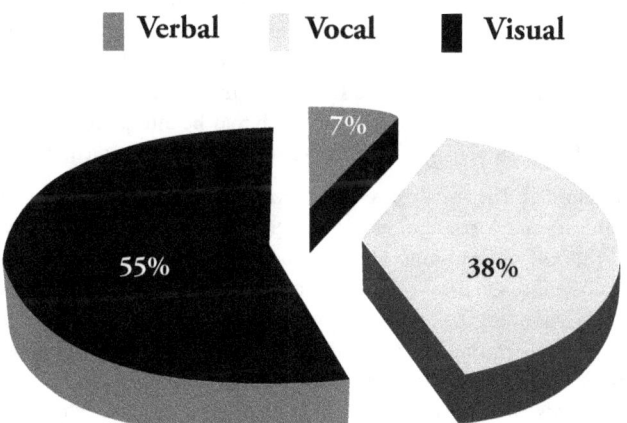

Verbal elements: Verbal communication involves the systematic arrangement of words to construct an idea and transmitting it through utterances. The choice of the words (diction) that the speaker uses determines the message meaning and the impact. Well-chosen words can effectively convey the intended meaning while ambiguity can mislead the recipients. Similarly, use of qualifiers such as big, good, excellent, courageous and perfect can influence the interpretation of message by the audience. Keep in mind that this element has the least impact overall.

Vocal elements: Vocal communication revolves around the elements of etiquette, rhythm, tone and intonation. They determine whether the yield of a dialogue is satisfactory or not. Etiquette deals with the degree of responsiveness to the accepted social code of conduct – otherwise referred to as good manners. It may also include adherence to the customary order of the dominant community. For example, in many communities there is the prescribed way in which elders should address children, women and the youth and vice versa. Regardless of the position that the communicator occupies, it is often not a choice but an obligation to use the code accepted by the community. The rhythm is simply the pace of utterances. Tone is the quality or the character of the vocal sound while intonation is the variation in pitch within the connectedness of a speech. The vocal elements of tone and intonation bear the biggest role in message delivery. This is because both denote the communicator's attitude towards the subject and the audience. For example, a positive statement in a speech may be interpreted to imply the opposite of what is stated by analysing the tone or the intonation of the speaker.

Visual elements: The visual expressions have the biggest impact on programme communication. Most often, within communication circles, visual elements denote the use of emotions or nonverbal cues. The latter includes facial expressions, gestures, dress code, voice nuances, body posture, attentiveness, presence, responding to others nonverbal cue and other body movements. Visibility of programmatic activities too forms the visual component of communication. Thus the popular phrase 'actions speak louder than words'. In other words, how the message is shared matters more than what is shared. All these can be summarised as the body language. Body language can send thousands of cues in one minute, which are sometimes difficult to manage. In a written text, the visual element may include the neatness of the work, the style of presentation and packaging. The Visual contributes 55% of the meaning. In the programme communication context for instance, how stakeholders perceive the individuals behind the programme communication significantly influences the success or failure of it. Perception of positive attitude promotes cohesion and team work. Negative destroys these.

The dialogical case below simulates a programme communication process and highlights the impact on the 3Vs in the communication process.

Mahat convenes a staff meeting to introduce a new internet access product – a light version new browser designed to offer three main benefits to the programme: promote efficiency in internal systems operation by ensuring fast internet; promote cost efficiency by regulating the bandwidth use within the programme and enhance security of data in the electronic data management systems:

Mahat: Good morning guys, thanks for convening. Today I have good news for you, but not too good if you are the kind of person who spends much of your time connected to community beyond the office perimeter wall during working hours.

(Mahat takes the team through the new version of the browser, every one listening carefully. Occasionally discussing as he illustrates the access processes).

Abdullahi: Excuse me Mahat! When do you expect the new system to be up and running?

Mahat: Monday next week! By 8.00 am, you won't be able to access the internet through the usual versions. I will send the log-in details to your emails over the weekend.

Abdullahi: Well…..that sounds good! How different is the new browser from the usual market versions. In other words, what is new?

Mahat: Not much different, but to access internet, you have to use a password. That way we will be able to monitor usage of internet within the programme.

Abdullahi: So, why the effort in using a password to access a new system while I can simply click and access now without it?

Mahat: For you, not so much difference, only additional responsibility, but for the programme ..... Yes. There is a big difference. We spend huge sum of money on internet.

Abdullahi: So what does expenditure on internet concern me! (Agitated)

Mahat: As I said, it may be insignificant to you, but for the programme it is not. Most staff spend half of the official working time in the social media...and...and streaming.

Abdullahi: (he meditates ... the working environment here is terrible, gunshots each hour, someone has died today, someone was injured yesterday, and still tomorrow, not sure what is in the offing, not television access for news and updates, loneliness, workload, bad food ...and this fool thinks we are here to misuse internet!).
He speaks out, 'so does the management think that we do not know what we are employed to do?'

Mahat: Not really, it's a normal process. We are rolling out this system globally. But this office is a priority. We spend a lot of internet here! (Abdullahi picks his Smartphone, logs in a chat page and ignores Mahat presentation henceforth).

Ken: So, do you want to monitor whatever we do over the internet?
Mahat: Not actually, we will only restrict access to the essential sites.

Ken: How do you determine which is essential and not?

Mahat: Simple!! (Systematically folding his figures) YouTube out, Facebook out, Porn sites out, other video sites out, filthy content sites out.... We are an ethical organization and we have to uphold best practices.

Ken: So what is your value addition in our day to day work!

Mahat: A lot of benefits; fast access to internet, fast download of documents, faster emails, minimal crashing of system, mitigated virus risks, name them...

Edna: The internet is already too slow!

Mahat: You guys make it slow!

Edna: Why can't you provide higher capacity bandwidth?

Mahat: We have the best internet available in the country. I do not carry internet in my pockets!

Edna: Offended, she shuts up and switches off!

Kimondiu: So what is the probability that the new system will succeed!

Mahat: It must succeed; the management has invested a lot in it, hiring a consultant, training HQ staff and everything. Furthermore, beginning next week, the normal system will be shut down. Only this new browser will be functioning in your computers.

Kimondiu: (In low utterance) Shit, let's see.

Applicability of the 3Vs determinant

Verbal: Through the presentation, Mahat addresses the key objectives of introducing the new access portal; to promote cost efficiency, enhance internet speed and promote electronic data system security. He however does not systematically organize the presentation to bring out the benefits and gain the buy in of the meeting participants, as he immediately begins by showing how disadvantaged the team would be as their access to internet would not only be controlled, but privacy will be compromised.

Visual: A distinctive aspect of this case is that the mood set at the introduction of the subject matter is negative and in response the team becomes combative. Mahat does not make things better as he continues to show that whatever the opinion of others it does not matter, the decision has been made and the team has to adopt or shift out. His body language too speaks a thousand words as he lists sites that are inadmissible in the programme, which seem to portray the team as morally unsuitable to work for the programme. The expectation should therefore not be that the same team should implement the new system. Furthermore, access point has no value addition to the team members' work, beyond enhancing data security.

Vocal: An outstanding element of this case is that the Mahat clearly communicates the overlying reason behind the new system; it is a quota approach to bandwidth management. The other two reasons are subordinate to bandwidth management agenda;his motive overshadows the very other positive benefits the access point would offer. The reaction from the team is immediate. When Abdullahi says, 'well…..that sounds good!' it can clearly be deciphered that he means the opposite- that he is neither interested in the new access point nor does he believe it has value addition to his work. The same pattern of interpretation is evident from the reaction of the other participants. While responding to Edna's question, Mahat clearly dissociates with the experiences of the team by arguing that he does not carry internet in his pocket. The tone is unfriendly, combative and offensive and therefore he should not expect the team to implement the initiative. Indeed, Kimondiu indicates that the battle lines have been drawn. This situation could have been avoided by anticipating that the new access point disadvantages the users while benefiting the for programme and therefore the process should have begun with consultations, propping up the benefits, setting the proper mood and adopting positive attitude on the side of Mahat. Non combative, natural tone could help in setting the mood of the team members.

B). DEVELOPING RESULTS-BASED PROGRAMME COMMUNICATION STRATEGY.

In words of Kristen Wolf, 'communication is not an end. It can be a powerful means to changing hearts and minds…'(Wolf 2001). Complexity in programme communication comes in when managers think of the tactics first, rather than a strategy. This approach complicates things when the tactics get in contact with a changing or adversarial situation and are not applicable any more, and what follows is a series of aimless tactics. Consequently, the programme heads into a landmine! Programme communication tactics such as media brief, media advocacy messages, stakeholders forums etc. are value additives only if they contribute to the programme communication overall goal defined in a communication strategy.

A programme pommunication strategy development encompasses THREE main steps:

1. Carrying out needs assessment/diagnosis
2. Planning and designing of the Strategy
3. Implementing, monitoring and evaluating progress

B.1 CARRY OUT NEEDS ASSESSMENT/DIAGNOSIS

The needs assessment provides a foundation for all other decisions made regarding the development and implementation of a programme communication strategy. Two levels of assessments are recommended: The general situation assessment and an in-depth assessment.

General Situation Assessment
It entails general analysis of the prevailing internal and external programme communication environments as shown in the chart in the next page.

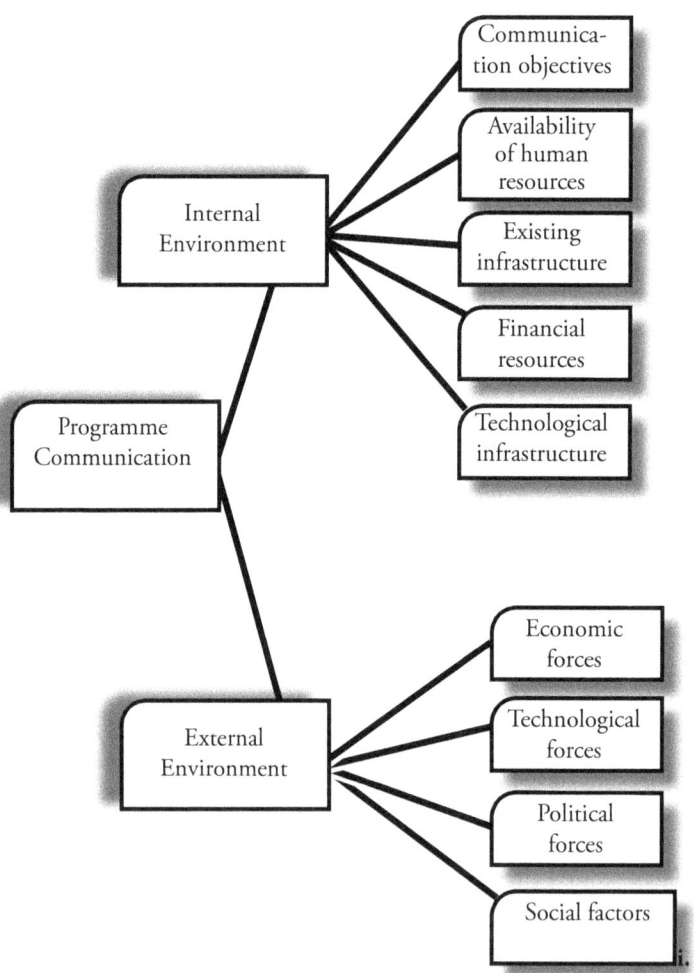

i. Scanning the Internal Environment

a. Communication Objectives: If there is no existing guide to a strategic programme communication plan, establishing one should be a priority. Other issues include whether team members are aware of the programme communication objectives: - if at all a strategy exists, and their influence on their responsibilities in making this objective happen. Also important to assess is whether there is a mechanism for the members to give input or feedback about the communication strategy and the programme as a whole.

b. Availability of Human Resource: Programmes often grapple with staff turnover and technology changes. Planning should consider what skills pool exists within the team, any additional training needed, whether there are volunteers for the programme and the cost of additional staffing if needed to scale up the existing capacities.

c. Existing Infrastructure: Whether there is a conducive office space(well lit, with power supply, internet network signals and security within the neighbourhood for staff and space for expansion etc., should influence the nature of the decisions made, particularly on financial resource allocation.

d. Financial Resources: Programme communication strategy requires strengthening of not just information dissemination processes but also the human and physical infrastructure. As such planning should be based on proper evaluation of the programme capacity to cater for the costs. This level of assessment is focused on identifying whether there is a laid down plan for financial resource allocation for the related human and physical infrastructure.

e. Technological Infrastructure: Availability of enough computers, software, high-speed connectivity system, and other physical equipment that support the technology should be assessed.

ii. Scanning the External Environment

a. Identification of the economic forces within the Society: This involves identification of the key movers of the stakeholders' information consumption behaviour. The composition of the society is clearly examined. For instance, 60% of the Kenyan population is made up of the youth. What are the behavioural characteristics of this demographic group? Does the communication target men or women? What are the characteristics of men within the society, and other groups? Identify the external sources of financial resources for the programme. If a non- governmental organization, how does the donor community view the organization and what are the future financial implications? If in business, what are the key products that support the profits and their competitive sustainability?

b. Technological Forces: In the rapidly changing technological environment, identification of latest trends should be of paramount importance. Identification of the latest products in online technology is not sufficient. The value comes in when the impact of the products in the whole information and communication strategy is used to place the programme strategically for imminent change, i.e. investment in technology, training of staff, recruitment of new technically able staff, sourcing of technical assistance, etc.

c. Political Forces: Political forces involve economic policies, investment policies, and the government's holistic development framework. For instance, the Kenya Vision 2030 forms an axis for economic, technological and social development. The framework has influenced the development of ICT infrastructure. Understanding the position of the programme in complementing the political vision and mission as well as effective adoption of changes is healthy. Political forces may favour programming or they may not. Thus, programme managers should anticipate the best and worst scenarios while investing in policy based processes.

e. Social-economic Forces: The social and cultural trends within a community determine the viability of a communication strategy. In other words, what is the mood of the society? Identify the latest interests and fears. The effective utilization of opportunities provided by social cultural changes is good for sustained growth.

In-depth Assessments

It is an elaborate process involving exploring issues and answering pertinent questions by analysing data. The data may be in quantitative form – numbers/figures or in qualitative – worded text or quotes. Credibility of data collected must first be ascertained to ensure that the ultimate strategy developed is actionable. This data is used to lay a foundation for progressive evaluation after the strategy is developed and operationalised. Some of the communication data collection methods include;

- Content\documents review: This involves scrutinizing information in the organizational records such as records, emails, memos, performance appraisals, job descriptions, and monthly or yearly reports for internal stakeholders and media articles (print, electronic and internet) for external stakeholders. Content review provides a good basis for evaluating past evidence of programme communication and data that cannot be retrieved by using other methods.

- Interviews: These may include one-on-one, structured or unstructured conversations with the programme stakeholders. This method is very important in that it allows one to gather sufficient qualitative data and probe for responses from the stakeholders. Since the data collection principally focuses on stakeholders'communication behaviour, unstructured conversations provide the most objective assessment of the prevailing situation. Structured or one-on-one interviews results may not always be all positive as stakeholders may be reluctant to provide information or provide misleading information which compromises the validity of the data collected.

- Focus group discussions: The stakeholders are engage in small structured group meetings where discussions on the programme communication behaviour take place. Their opinion is sought regarding measures necessary in developing and implementing a communication strategy that would bring forth utmost benefit to them and the programme. This process benefits from possible professional input of some of the stakeholders. The groups can also be useful in pretesting some of the identified strategy options.

- Surveys: Surveys are becoming popular with the advent of online tools that facilitate virtual connection of stakeholders. Other channels may however be expensive particularly if the stakeholders are thinly distributed. Surveys are useful in that they provide quantitative data which provides a strong foundation for analysing other qualitative information. These surveys can also be used to gather qualitative data – respondents detailed response on the survey questions.

- Observation: It is probably the most useful method as human senses can be deployed to assess the stakeholder communication behaviour in relation to the context: - social situation, natural setting and responsibilities. Observation may include self-report or data-asking the stakeholders what they do and comparing their feedback with what is directly observed. In situations where the person collecting the data has a limited. interaction with the stakeholders, use of recording devices may be useful. However, this tool has ethical implication if consent is not sought. Observation templates or coding sheets are useful in recording observed communication behaviour. It should however be noted that the templates or coding sheets may constrict data collection to the anticipated behaviour and therefore diligence to other important phenomena should be kept.

It is always preferable to use a combination of the above methods as this provides a diversity of the data collected, which helps in analysing various patterns of programme communication behaviour. The data is triangulated to;

- Derive the prevailing programme communication behaviours
- Analyze the needs of various stakeholders and map the resources available.
- Set the desired/target situation.
- Derive options likely to be adopted by the largest segment of the stakeholders.
- Set the scope of possible initiatives.
- Derive approaches that support the short, medium and long-term programme communication goals.
- Identify channels that will most conveniently and cost-effectively reach the internal and external stakeholders.
- Develop performance indicators - the expected stakeholders communication pattern/actions that indicate progress towards the desired/target situation.

It is important to compile a status report articulating the baseline data for use as reference source when measuring progress towards the desired situation; document the data in both qualitative and quantitative formats to act as a baseline for measuring progress.

B.2 DESIGN THE STRATEGY

One of the biggest challenges in programme communication strategy design is overcoming uncertainties in changing contexts. This is because human beings have a natural fear for change especially when the change is unpredictable. Therefore a simple strategy with greater impact has a higher chance of success than a fancy strategy that may lead to unforeseen risks, duplication of efforts and ineffective deployment of resources.

While carrying out the needs assessment/diagnosis process you identified a number of challenges that have hindered effective programme communication in the past, some success stories and most importantly key recommendations from the internal and external stakeholders that can help either overcome the challenges or build on the achievements made. This is the first point of reference for the development of the programme communication strategy.

Furthermore, while exploring the determinants of a good communication strategy earlier, several communication models were extrapolated. These determinants should form the second point of reference when designing the strategy. In addition, in this sub-section, a new theory of communication that would guide in the translation of the aggregated preferred option into a usable programme communication strategy will be introduced: - the Competing Values Framework for Corporate Communication (CVFCC). This model was developed by Cameron Kim and Quinn Robert in 2006 and emphasizes on strategic communication planning. The model is moulded around the interests of internal and external stakeholders or factors, while flexibility and control prevail within the managerial levels

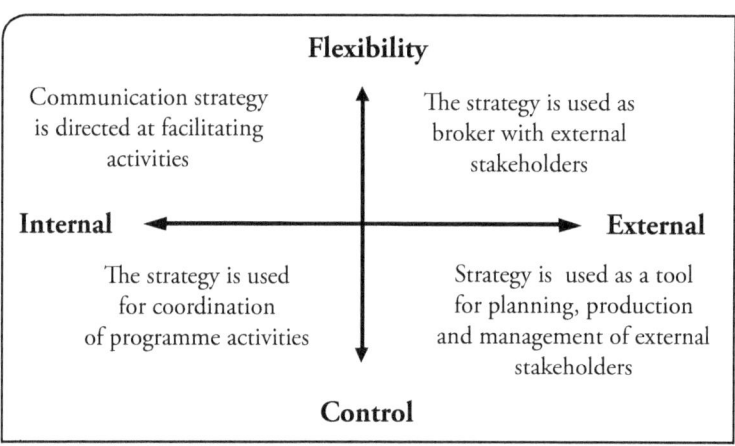

Flexibility

Communication strategy
is directed at facilitating
activities

The strategy is used as
broker with external
stakeholders

Internal ← → **External**

The strategy is used
for coordination
of programme activities

Strategy is used as a tool
for planning, production
and management of external
stakeholders

Control

Establishing a programme communication strategy is an evolving process involving, in some instances, dealing with issues with competing tensions and values. It involves identifying areas of strengths and gaps in communication strategy to be sealed and developing filling-in interventions while working to improve on existing areas of strength to boost effectiveness. The idea of competition not only involves external factors but also establishing a mechanism of decision making based on competing values and programme communication interventions.

In the opinion of Cameron and Quinn, the dominant operational theory that drives success is that competing creates an impetus for higher levels of productivity and therefore higher levels of effectiveness . Programme managers, in many instances, are faced with a wide operational field and are thus pressed by the need to focus on the important stakeholders in a manner that enhances sustainability of productivity towards achievement of the set goals. Strategic focus on two competing sides: - the internal and external side - provide a complex system, which cuts into a puzzle for managers particularly when they are required to strike a balance between the two sides. If this situation manifests, the CVFCC comes in as handy in developing a competitive communication strategy capable of effectively mobilizing resources inherent in the internal and external stakeholders, developing and guiding the manifestations of the desired programme communication behaviour. The chart below demonstrates the usability of CVFCC in programme communication strategy development:

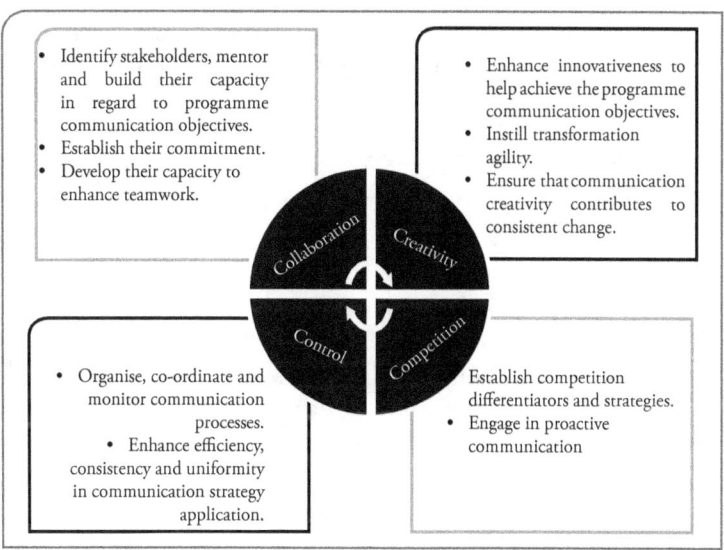

- Identify stakeholders, mentor and build their capacity in regard to programme communication objectives.
- Establish their commitment.
- Develop their capacity to enhance teamwork.

- Enhance innovativeness to help achieve the programme communication objectives.
- Instill transformation agility.
- Ensure that communication creativity contributes to consistent change.

- Organise, co-ordinate and monitor communication processes.
- Enhance efficiency, consistency and uniformity in communication strategy application.

Establish competition differentiators and strategies.
- Engage in proactive communication

The CVFCC enables development of an insightful communication strategy that builds and sustains strong programme communication practices. Therefore developing an indepth understanding of it contributes to innovative communication strategies that are adoptive to changes and responsive to trends and events. The framework provides a platform for developing an insightful system, in line with programme goals, mission, values, and culture. The framework-based plan is developed by first identifying the stakeholders' level of participation in the programme, performance, communication roles, and individualized communication traits to identify gaps and develop a more comprehensive and inclusive strategy for promoting both inter and intra personal communication.

In addition, it helps the programme manager to develop an information dissemination regulatory framework that ensures that information flows in a structural manner and in line with the people's culture, behaviour, and social values. Based on the framework, programme communication focuses on identity, compliance with the programme missions, visions, and values and uniformity. Within this framework, effective communication is based on identification of the unique requirements associated with varied communication domains and targeting all areas of intervention. This helps in developing response mechanisms that effectively utilize communication channels. In view of the above, the following should be observed when designing a communication strategy:

1.Creativity

The data collected at the assessment stage provides a picture of the prevailing situation and a good source of vantage points that if critically analysed provide creative and preferable options to programme communication. How should one know that the strategy being developed is innovative?

The first pointer for creativity lies in understanding the target situation and how each option contributes to transformation of the programme communication practices/behaviour towards the desired outcomes.

The second pointer is how the preferred options instil transformation agility among the stakeholders? Stakeholders have varied behavioural approaches to communication and in most cases each stakeholder looks for what would benefit them in the communication cycle or in the programme as a whole. Yet, the strategy should have an inherent capacity to motivate each stakeholder to proactively and innovatively adopt behaviours that are in perspective with the communication strategy.

The last pointer is that the strategy should accommodate innovation. The existing approaches may fail to materialize because of increased competing interests and contextual dynamics. Regardless of these challenges, the focus should remain the target situation. New approaches that adapt to the changing situation should be adopted on continuous basis. The communication strategy should ensure sustained effectiveness in communication and productivity, all contributing to achievement of the targeted performance matrices.

2. Competition

A programme communication strategy should build on lessons learned from previous strategies either within the organization or in other organizations. Some fundamental questions that if properly answered can shade some light on unique elements that make a strategy competitive include:

- Is there an existing communication strategy?
- If yes, what are the successes and limitations?
- What strategies from other related programmes internally or externally exist that can be used for comparison purposes?
- How successful have they been?
- Can their successes be considered fair and relevant benchmarking options?
- What are their limitations?
- How different should the new strategy be?
- How different should the programme communication strategy?

To remain competitive, it is important to anticipate the communication needs of stakeholders and try to meet them. The programme communication strategy should therefore provide guidance towards this end:

The strategy should clearly outline the objectives of programme communication and the methodology of achieving them. For instance, if it is intended to inform and persuade a specific tier of stakeholder such as financiers, the objectives may revolve around continuous analysis of the changing operational context and sharing the information with them to influence their priorities, win their acceptance of the programme or adjustment to existing programme and at the same time magnify the programme image.

- The strategy should clearly identify the range of programme stakeholders to determine the nature of messages that should be disseminated.

- The strategy should identify and promote use of the most appropriate communication channels. For instance, continuously sharing email communication to stakeholders or use of memos is monotonous and not suitable in some situations. Other options such as a surprise telephone call to the stakeholders or use of new media multimedia platforms such as Skype could promotes stakeholder satisfaction, build closer working relationships and interpersonal relationships which have longer lasting positive impact on the programme.

3. Collaboration

Stakeholders have different levels of influence and therefore it is important to provide stakeholders' prioritization criteria in the strategy. This allows for direction of specific communication where it has the biggest positive impact on the programme. Information needs may either be founded on policy (often detailed in partnership agreements), formally or informally requested by stakeholders and therefore regular sharing of relevant programme communication enhances positive working relationship.

4. Control

The strategy should provide guidelines on how to control programme communication. These guidelines should include:

- The message
- The periodicity of communication
- How to package the communication
- The channels for transmitting the communication.

For example, if the programme supports several projects, chances are that several staff or partners have been deployed to implement the projects, yet these different projects should contribute to a single overarching objective. In this situation, the periodicity of sharing of information to and from those implementing the projects should be spelled out, ensure that timelines, instructions and guidelines are clear and promote uniformly in provision of data. This ensures that only relevant information is gathered from the various implementers, and at the same time promotes ease of compilation of these inputs into a single high quality document. The communication should make use of channels that reach out to the recipients efficiently.

Depending on the number of projects in a programme, effective control entails being able to know the specific details of each project, establishing a proper archiving system, filing, record of the relevant communication templates and tracking systems such as documents tracker, projects tracker, financial tracker etc. Once these are in place, coordination of information dissemination is made easier, as source documents (contracts, project documents, work plans, etc.) and templates can easily be retrieved. The tracking systems allow for regular monitoring of progress of each project.

Designing of the strategy involves evaluating the available options for the strategy against the envisioned best case scenario; on the available insightful data; evaluating the possible consequence of the available option; and choosing the combination of options which have a preferred results relative to the programme overall strategy.

This combination of preferred options should exhibit:

i. Responsiveness: The options should accommodate the needs of different stakeholders. This ensures that the strategy fits into or promotes the overall strategic goal of the programme by identifying the scope within which all initiatives shall be carried out.

The main factors to consider include:

- Closely consulting with the stakeholders who are expected to play a role the implementation of the strategy. This is important in that it provides a platform for critical evaluation of proposed elements of the preferred set of options and allows for correction of mistakes that if not detected at the designing stage may affect the subsequent stages of development and ultimate failure of the final strategy.
- The available resources that can be tapped to develop the communication strategy. Sharing a summary of the key recommendations from the assessment/diagnosis process with the key programme and support stakeholders creates a good platform for tapping on the wealth of experience among the internal stakeholders. For example, each department would assess the implications of the draft recommendations to their operation and possibly propose a focal point person who would closely work with the communication strategist to ensure that the best interests all other stakeholders within the department are considered. These focal persons act as a reference group and promote interrativity (refer to Scramm model of communication discussed earlier in part 4 of this book) throughout the strategy development process.

ii. Thoughtfulness: Taking time either as an individual or a group to discuss and analyse different ideas available ensures that the options chosen are warranted and few or no mistakes are made. Ultimately, the strategy should include the methods of identifying whether the identified options contribute to the overall strategic goal (the key performance indicators).

ii. Sensitivity to other people's needs: The stakeholders should not be coerced to accept and adopt the strategy if they are rationally opposed to it. Consensus should first be established on contentious issues. It is best if the strategy is developed in a manner that respects the people's culture, emphasizes on and respects the positive relationships and behaviours as guided by the cultural values, within the society.

iv. Comprehensive technical consultation: There should be sufficient experts' input in the development process. If necessary, the programme manager can contract a consultant with vast experience in developing such strategies, and has clear knowledge of the social values of the society.

v. Effective resolution of problems when they arise: This avoids unnecessary delays due to conflicts between the affected parties and the strategy development agents.

vi. Cost Efficient: The set of preferred options should be those that deliver the greatest impact at reasonable cost. This includes the cost of direct implementation, the human resource and infrastructure development.

The main deliverables at this level are represented in the chart below;

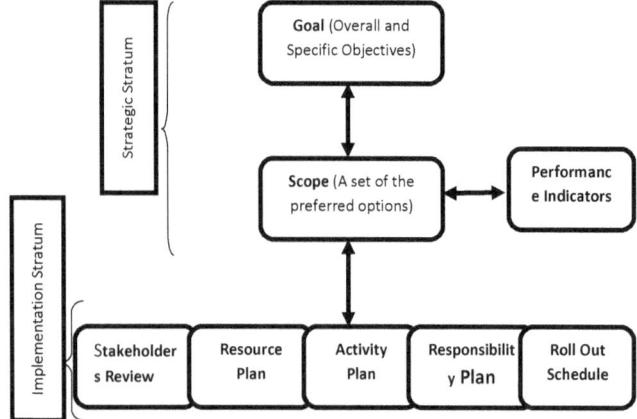

This primarily involves identification of the goal (which also includes identification of the specific objectives) and the scope (a set of the preferred options) of the programme communication strategy. The stratum involves first detailing the programme communication goal and logically deriving the specific objectives. This section is the most important as the goal and the objectives should sufficiently respond to the aggregated preferred option (s) derived after needs assessment/diagnosis. It is a decision making process that looks at both the significance of the proposed objectives and the consequence within competing values (the need to uphold standards in communication - including efficiency, inclusiveness, relevance and predicatbility - refer to part three of this book) and stakeholders contexts (the need to meets the communication needs of the diversity of both internal and external stakeholders without compromising the development and implementation of the programme as a whole).

During the identification of the scope of the strategy, the 20/80 principle comes in handy. In other words, the process should focus on the 20% most important deliverables to deliver 80% of the intended results. The combination of options should be that which generates the preferred set of consequences to the programme. Key performance indicators may be pegged on each of the preferred option to ensure that measurement of achievements towards the set communication goal is made possible.

Case Illustration 5: The Strategic Stratum for the strategy

Goal: Promote effective, relevant, inclusive and predictable results based programme communication.	
Specific Objectives	1.To overcome foreseeable obstacles to effective programme implementation. 2. Promote inclusiveness in programme decision making processes. 3. Promote programme communication culture that consistently contributes to the short, medium and long term goals. 4. To enhance the relevant cost effective communication infrastructure.
Scope/Key Deliverables 1: Internal Stakeholders	1a. 1b. 1c. 1d.
2: External Stakeholders	2a. 2b. 2c. 2d

THE IMPLEMENTATION STRATUM

This section concerns the tools necessary for execution of the communication strategy.

i. The Stakeholders Review:

This tool provides basic guidelines for engagement with both internal and external stakeholders. It is founded on a critical review of the composition of the stakeholders to identify their role in the programme implementation and for some, the behavioural and socio-cultural aspects that may influence their communication behaviour. It entails being knowledgeable of the attitudes, identities, history, behaviour, culture, social system, and perceptions of all stakeholders towards the programme.

Many societies have more than one language used; they have the official language, the national languages or the languages of the majority and minorities. In most cases use of the official or national language is preferred when developing a programme communication strategy. However, in other cases these official languages are not used by all members of the society and therefore understanding the linguistic orientation of each stakeholder is an important ingredient of the project communication strategy. Programme communication may be presented in more than one language, particularly when developing operational visibility materials and when using the mass media to reach out to stakeholders who are spread across expansive geographic locations.

It is important to note that every stakeholder (individual) has;

- A culture defined by the language of their native society and with a distinct code system that defines the meaning of things.

- Social attributes that influences inter-personal communication behaviour.

- Individual perception influenced by experience within a cultural context.

- Moral values relative to the cultural and societal narrative that guides how they communicate.

Also note the following basic facts about stakeholders:

- They do not hold a fixed opinion all the time.

- They are not fixed in number. New stakeholders may emerge after the strategy is rolled out, with fresh information needs.

- Their circumstances may change within the programme period and demand more information; such as accountability.

Each stakeholder has specific information needs, preferred channel of communication and periodicity. The programme communication strategy should detail these details with the objective of building mutually benefiting collaboration with the stakeholders. It should also contain a stakeholders' matrix containing details of each stakeholder.

Although there are various ways to develop stakeholders' matrix, the following table exemplifies a typical tool that can be used to develop this matrix:

Stakeholder (s)	Title	Contact	Message	Frequency	Media	Responsible

The stakeholders column should contain correct naming of the stakeholders, be it individuals, or groups. The second column should contain accurate titles. The third column should contain one or more of the contacts of the stakeholders; in most cases, physical address, email address and telephone numbers are included in this column. You do not have to write in advance what you will communicate to stakeholders; this section requires an outline in few points of the information that the stakeholders need and how the information should be disseminated; precautions to be taken when disseminating the information may also be included. Frequency column details when the information should be disseminated e.g., monthly, quarterly, at or before a specific stage of rolling out activities. The media column details the most appropriate medium of communication for each stakeholder e.g e-mail, stakeholder meeting, broadcast media, new media platforms etc. The responsible column lists the person/department, within the internal stakeholders; or if in a partnership, among the partners who should disseminate the information to the targeted stakeholders.

All communication actions should be directed towards achieving the agreed upon programme goal. However, this is only possible when the stakeholders understand how they directly or indirectly contribute to the programme goal. For example, if one of the objectives is to promote accountability to stakeholders through timely and accurate information gathering and dissemination, the programme manager should know that initiatives such as stakeholders participation particularly in the provision of, validation of key data and pretesting of the information are important element in promoting accountability. Other means may include enabling the stakeholders, if relevant, to participate in activities such as needs assessment, periodic information sharing forums or other avenues deemed appropriate. Regular feedback and timely response to stakeholders concerns and providing clarification where there is a misunderstanding should be embraced to enhance mutual understanding of the programme deliverables.

Some stakeholders may not have the required capacity to effectively support the programme information/communication needs. The programme communication strategy should anticipate this situation and provide for allocation of sufficient resources to develop the capacities of the stakeholder. Capacity development may take the form of training, provision of communication equipment or recruitment of relevant human resource.

Example One: Internally, to electronically archive relevant communication documents the programme team requires proper equipment such as Computer servers, high capability scanners, reliable internet access etc. These form the enabling infrastructure and require resource allocation when making programme budgets. The software element of capacity building may involve training on use of the equipment, development and capacity building of the staff on proper electronic archiving systems and maintenance of the infrastructure. Externally, stakeholders' support may involve provision of funding to hire the relevant human resource or establishment of the relevant infrastructure.

Example Two: A government office without a printer is not expected to provide the necessary documentation or communication to facilitate implementation of a programme. Provision of support in procurement of a good printer and complementary materials and equipment such as cartridge and computers would go a long way in enabling programme communication. Articulating the circumstances in which this support can be provided and clear resource allocation guidelines promote both internal and external stakeholders communication.

ii. Resource Plan

This tool details a critical assessment of both the human and financial resources required to operationalise the preferred set of options that form the scope of the strategy. Sometimes it may not be possible to realistically breakdown the actual cost of the strategy. Other times it may be possible. It all depends on either the complexity or simplicity of the selected options. However, the basic factor is that detailing the broader level cost estimates may help in initial process of resource mobilization.

iii. Activity Plan:

This should be the list of activities that should be carried out or messages that should be disseminated for the stated objectives to be achieved. If necessary a breakdown of the budget estimate for the activity can be included. This helps in assessing the cost efficiency in implementing each activity. It may not be possible to provide finer details of the activities that would be carried out to achieve the communication objective, but a broader details of the key interventions is helpful in shading some light on the key interventions and the subsequent deliverables, which should be measurable within the laid down performance indicators. Some of the broader level activities may include;

- Strengthening interpersonal communication within the internal and external stakeholders
- Establishing an archiving system of programme communication documents
- Establishing a reliable communication infrastructure
- Ongoing reinforcement of the best communication practices
- External stakeholders mapping
- Development of advocacy messages
- Development of programme communication templates
- Developing programme visibility guidelines

iv. Responsibility Plan

The overall responsibility of programme communication rests on the programme manager. However, as the other members of the programme team are more often in day to day implementation of programme activities than the manager; it is essential to identify the sections of communication plan that can be handled by the programme implementation team members, and those that need the support of communication specialists, or the senior programme management team. Division of roles can also be guided by the overall programme implementation plan in that the persons implementing specific activities acquire the required skills and adopt the best approaches to execute the core matter of the intervention and therefore strategic communication needs to act as a lever for the implementation of the programme activities.

v.   Roll Out Schedule

This is simply the order of implementation of the strategic communication initiatives. The timing for most of the initiatives related to direct programme implementation would most likely be guided by the programme implementation schedule. However, other activities which touch on internal and external communication not related to the schedule of programme activities should be sequentially organised such that activities that are dependent on accomplishment of others follow the independent interventions, while those which support the success of the independent interventions come before these actions. This schedule also helps in monitoring of the progress towards the achievement of programme communication objectives.

C. ROLLING OUT THE PROGRAMME COMMUNICATION STRATEGY

Rolling out programme communication strategy is simply operationalising it. It involves the actual exchange of information on programme issues. Progress towards a results based programme communication occurs in a continuum and therefore the roll out process should be systematic and regularly evaluated to measure the milestones covered and build on the lessons learned from the preceding phase of implementation. Regular evaluation should assess how the strategy contributes to the achievement of the programme communication objectives and subsequently the programme goal. To make this possible, effort should be made to ensure that new and creative ideas promote consistent change and in a manner that promote the programme short, medium and long- term goals.

There are many ways to roll out a programme communication strategy. However, in this section focus will be made on two dimensions; the human and system dimensions.

C.1 THE HUMAN DIMENSION

This dimension rests on the pretext that all actors in programme communication are human beings and would basically want to be treated as such at all times. Either individually or collectively, they form the internal or external stakeholders. As stakeholders they are diverse in that their approach to communication is mentored by each individual's basic orientation to humanity.

Therefore take note of the following attributes:
- We need each other to be human.
- We have shared values as human beings.
- We differ in taste and preferences.
- We are influenced more often by our social cultural background than reason.
- Isolation brings about destructive anxieties, insecurities and paranoia that affects how we socialize and communicate with others.
- Each human being has elements of egocentrism, individualism and materialism.
- Our wants may not necessarily be sensitive to the needs of others.

- Not everyone is concerned about the public good.
- The basic public policy when aggressed is retribution.
- You cannot distinctively separate perception and communication.
- Love, mercy, compassion and generosity are positive attribute that influence how we value, share and use information.

These attributes also mirror the similarities and differences of the internal and external stakeholders, which should be considered when rolling out a programme communication strategy.

Some of the common similarities include:

No	Similarities
1.	Mutually beneficial relationships create a sense of belonging; promote responsiveness and how stakeholders' value and use programme communication for the common good.
2.	The stakeholders have a social-cultural background that influence how they reason, interpret meaning (Refer to the mediation by signs/semiotics model by Ferdinand de Saussure discussed in part 4) and provide feedback.
3.	Love, mercy, compassion and generosity are positive attribute that influence how the stakeholders value, share and use information.
4.	Perception and communication cannot be separated. Stakeholders communicate/interpret meaning as influenced by their world view or perception of the interlocutor- person communicating on behalf of the programme team.
5.	Each stakeholder has to some degree a personalized interest in the programme and if no evidence of benefit to each stakeholder, whether a member of programme team or an organization may not provide the support needed to effectively implement the programme communication strategy.

And,

the table below exemplifies some of the differences between internal and external stakeholders:

No.	Internal Stakeholders	External stakeholders
1.	Include general staff, middle line managers, senior managers, owners/ shareholders, board of directors	Include partners, beneficiaries, authorities, contractors, society, competitors, media etc.
2.	Have shared values i.e. education, language, office culture, purpose etc	No shared value: - are from different cultural background, do not always have shared purpose, may care less about others
3.	May have higher degree of self control when aggressed	The public policy of retribution when aggressed may become the first option
4.	Sense of isolation may easily bring about destructive anxieties, insecurities and mistrust which negatively affects the support some stakeholders provide to those perceived to isolate them.	Sense of isolation may lead to aggression, withdrawal of their support to programme.

Therefore, the diversity of the stakeholders and the intrinsic attributes should be considered while rolling out the programme communication strategy, whether for internal or external programmes.

C.2 THE SYSTEMS DIMENSION

The system dimension concerns putting in place the right communication infrastructure and identification of and effective use of communication channels. The hardware system include; computers, network connectivity gadgets, telephone and printers among others. The Software system is basically the communication strategy. Once the systems are in place, the next phase involves identification of the suitable communication channels:

Two classical channels to communication have often been used to roll out programme communication strategies and are commonly referred to as the traditional communication. These are the formal and informal channels.

A third channel, which will be discussed seperately and in detail in the proceeding sections is the new media.

Formal channels: They are often used when there is no close relationship between the two or more people and in circumstances under which the information is needed by or affects more than one stakeholder, mainly the recipient of the information. They include the following:

i. Group Meetings

Group meetings are useful only when proper atmosphere for participatory decision-making is established, especially in situations whereby the decisions affect the stakeholders directly. All-inclusive meeting should be held when the programme manager plans to advocate for major strategy change or reinforcement of the same, to enable the stakeholders to be part of the process and work as if they are achieving their personalized objectives. In some instances, to create the atmosphere necessary for free interaction and exchange it is advisable to introduce some aspects of informality. For example, focus group discussions in which personnel are guided to discuss varied issues of concern takes the formal form. Inversely, depending on how they are composed and the setting, focus group discussions can be informal forums for rolling out the strategy.

Benefits of Group Meetings
- Create a chance for the personnel to share ideas freely.
- Boost individual morale. An effective meeting facilitator can make everyone participate, even the most timid.

- The organization benefits from ideas that personnel could not share in a different set up.
- Creation of confidence of personnel enhances their input.
- Enhances team building. It can be a socialization activity especially when the venue invites a departure from the office atmosphere.

Note: The best meetings are those that the boss is not all time facilitator. Other talented members can be allowed to lead some agenda of the meetings after going through an appropriate capacity building process.

Drawbacks
- Poorly facilitated meetings may lead to conflicts, hindering decision making.
- Some problematic people may derail the main agenda.

ii. Stakeholders Briefing
This may be held either once per week or as deemed appropriate and may be determined by the activities of the programme and the core values. These help to keep the stakeholders updated on the programme successes and challenges and are suitable forums for reinforcing application of the best practices by the stakeholders.

iii. E-Mail
Electronic mail is an important channel in that it's relatively cheap to maintain and can reach out to selected stakeholders; and dissemination of the stakeholder specific information. Mails sent easily reach stakeholders within the shortest time possible.

iv. Memos
Memos are integral in formal programme communication and are often intended for groups. They convey general information for both internal and external audience. Internal memos are mainly pinned on the notice boards for everyone to read or sent through the internal mailing system. This channel is suitable for a communication intended to reinforce preferred behaviour, or correct an unfavourable practice. However, it can cause a sense of disquiet particularly because memos leave little room for stakeholders to offer their

input. It may therefore be necessary to first use one on one channel such as group or one-on-one meetings to give stakeholders opportunity to respond to the communication and then document the directives/communication through a memo, which reinforces what had been discussed through the meetings.

Informal channels: They are used when stakeholder communicate without stringent adherence to protocol. The level of equality among the stakeholders is high. In most instances, the stakeholders tend to work in groups or as a team. The informal communication channels help the decision makers and other stakeholders to gather information that may not be disseminated by the stakeholders through the formal channels.

i. Team lunches and sports activities
These provide an out-of-office atmosphere, necessary for interaction of the junior and senior personnel. The interaction is essential in that the senior personnel get to know about information that cannot be transmitted through the communication structures because of bureaucracy and censoring.

ii. Social gatherings
They are used by personnel within or outside the organization. The gatherings are mainly held to discuss emerging issues. The informal gatherings help personnel to exchange information and give out clues on information which is not officially released to them. Although the gatherings may be exposed to some misuse like acting as forums for rumours milling or organizing picketing activities or strikes, if well used they prepare the personnel to receive the information when communicated officially. They also avoid information shock among the personnel.

Literary, the above approaches can just be assumed to be the general processes of office communication. However, in programme communication it is important to project communication from the conventional approaches to tactical approaches. Conventional approaches here imply information dissemination without a conscious attention to intended goal. Tactical approach here implies evaluating the best options relative to the communication and information needs of the stakeholders. For example; convening a programme staff meeting to share information on a new data collection platform that will require then to provide data after every week may be a programmatically strategic idea, but has other dimensions; it is additional responsibility for the staff who may be already too overworked to meet the additional reporting needs. The tactical level may involve identifying the cost benefit of using the new system and collecting feedback from the staff on the most suitable frequency of reporting. Earlier on the need for flexibility in programme communication was discussed; collecting the views of the programme staff and aggregating them may bring about a compromise and change the cause of the initial plan; say to collect data within a periodicity of two weeks. This is obviously not the interest of the manager but it reflects a collective position and therefore the programme team is more likely to take responsibility in adhering to the agreed upon periodicity than mare obedience of the boss!

THE NEW MEDIA DRIFT

In Tsinghua University, on 15th December 2003, the world re-known entrepreneur and a Chinese National Li Ka Shing argued that 'Information and communications technology unlocks the value of time, allowing and enabling multitasking, multi- channels, multi-this and multi-that' (Shing 2005). These words focused on calling for a new way of thinking among the Chinese nationals and development of a new framework to enhance the national innovative vitality.

Today, millions of people are connected in the online interaction and communication platforms. So far, the main genera of the new media include: Websites, chat interfaces, cell phone interfaces, televised sports, digital video and games, interactive multimedia, blogs, multimedia presentations, museum kiosks, e-cards and hypertext novels, among others.

The new media differs from the old media in the channels of distribution, relationship between the media and the audience and the nature of message composition.

Sociologists have positively appraised the new media, as it has created a network as a complex system of interrelationships between people at all levels of society. For example, 72% of Lebanese connected through the mobile phones in 2013 used social networking sites (Wike and Oatesm 2013). The social networks connectivity rates are as low as 50% in most developing countries, yet this represent a significant proportion of the societies to warrant proper investment in the new media as a channel of programme communication. Regardless of the platform that new media users exploit to create and sustain the relationships, individuals are networked according to age, interests, and behaviour.

The managerial significance of the new media is documented in the Return on Investment (ROI) 2013-2014 study by Towers Watson which shows that managers who scored best in effective communication of strategies are three and a half times more likely to outperform their industry peers, as they possess a deep understanding of the community culture and behaviour (Towers 2014). Of the 56% respondents who reported using social media, those that used multiple approaches within the diversity of approaches reported bigger impact than those who used a single approach. Towers Watson is a leading global professional services company which publishes the Change and Communication ROI Study and has over the past 10 years carried out a bi-annual study on the relationship between change management, communication and performance.

Furthermore, the new media technology has enhanced the capability of people to create relationships with others they have not encountered before face-to-face. The core factor here is interest based relationships. The networks have created forums for interaction and alliances to accomplish particular objectives.

The increase in the numbers of users of the new media compels programme stakeholders and other influential institutions to strategically focus on using it to enhance both programmatic and institutional interests.

The new media technology has brought Internet communication to the masses at all levels: The political, economic, and the social levels. Some of the key players: ordinary citizens, civic organizations, political players, governments, private actors and all that seek to galvanize the masses' support on a wide set of issues have found the new media technology a handy tool for mobilizing those who are not reached by the mainstream media, and enhancing individualized reach to those reached through the mass media. Their activities span from competition to recruitment of more members to advocacy - 'seducing' the enrolled members to take an action against or in support of their positions/ agenda. In contemporary times, the public is increasingly developing trust in the new media as a source of trusted information. The success of the media has been documented in a number of events.

Example 1

President Barrack Obama, while a presidential candidate, used Facebook,

Twitter and MySpace to mobilize millions of followers through cell phones and computers. This played an important role in influencing the young undecided voters who often visited social sites. At the end of campaign, the campaign team had mobilized 6,267,981 supporters through the new media. The team Obama mastered the use of new media and technology not only as a tool for grassroot mobilising but also for fundraising (Alexandrova, 2010). The late awakening of the challenger John McCain enabled him to raise only 625,000 supporters by the close of the campaign. Obama's strategic team not only used the sites for membership support but also to raise the huge chunk of money that aided in the coordination of his campaign initiatives.

Example 2

In February 2008, Oscar Morales launched a Facebook campaign opposing terrorism activities of the Revolutionary Armed Forces of Colombia popularly known as the FARC rebels (Burstein 2012). Shortly after the launch groups of students across 185 cities march protested the acts of the rebels who had kidnapped people and kept them hostage for years in the jungle. The campaign was dubbed, 'Million Voices Against the FARC'. The catalysts in the campaigns were documents and videos posted on Facebook showing the hostages still alive but held in very harsh conditions. The appeal of the message to millions of people worldwide and subsequent outcry compelled the rebels to immediately release all hostages. The global march was extensively aired through the mainstream media, mainly by the British Broadcasting Corporation (BBC), CNN, the New York Times, El Tiempo, the Colombian national daily and other international media. The campaign gained such great momentum that the FARC Rebels' pro-reform campaign was reversed and replaced with defensive strategies.

Example 3

In January 2011, the Tunisian President Ben Ali resigned after concerted efforts of demonstrators bore fruits. This set the stage for pro-democracy movements in the Arabic Nations. The Tunisia political landscape change was followed by Internet mobilization of Egyptians led by the one-time Director of the International Atomic Energy Agency (IAEA) Dr. Mohamed ElBaradei. Through the month of January, the nation experienced mass movements across the streets of Cairo and other major cities. Consequently, the long serving president went into exile. This revolution of mind was brought about by Internet power to mobilize the masses.

How do New Media promote programme communication?

The new media has a snow ball effect which supplies a nearly infinitive number of potential stakeholders (Joseph 2008). Therefore programme communication practitioners shall inevitably be more engaged in the new media in the coming years. Why this? A study conducted by UNOCHA 'Humanitarianism in the Network Age in 2012 illustrates the depth at which the mobile technology has offered an orthodoxy kick to the traditional top bottom approaches to creating and dissemination of information. 'The Internet and mobile technology continues to transform the way data is generated, collected and shared' (UN OCHA 2012). The increased coverage of internet and mobile connectivity has pushed the costs down, and will inevitably promote greater access to among the poorer people living in the rural, and in some instances difficult to access areas. The 2013 global attitude survey on mobile phone coverage and usage shows that 90% of Lebanese access internet daily, 84% for Jordan and use this platform to share information or give their opinion on topical issues. Of the 24 nations surveyed more than half used internet daily (Wike and Oates 2014). The UNOCHA report predicts that more than 50% world population will be covered by internet connectivity by 2015.

The most powerful way that the new media platform has influenced programme communication has been through 'crowdsourcing ' (Ibid) a phenomenon in which programme actors have been compelled to gather information from people in difficult to access disasters affected areas. The approach has also been used to validate data on delivery of aid and assess its effectiveness. Therefore, the beneficiaries are no longer timid recipients of assistance but a voice that shapes the opinion of policy and decision makers. In countries which lack strong institutions like Somalia for example, the mobile connectivity has served as a channel for aid delivery.

Then, there is another increasing use of new media, which is also gaining momentum in programme communication; measuring whether real life image equals offline image (perception). This has brought into focus another component; the Stakeholders Relations Management (SRM), which requires special skills. SRM is not optional in the growing new media user spectrum but a proactive process that involves sharing of answers with other stakeholders both internally and externally, solving their problems, and building reliable relationships.

The advent of new media has brought on board distinct capabilities in programme communication:

- Ubiquity: Is the new media capability of being everywhere, providing accessibility of the information and negating the physical restrictions like distance.

- Global Reach: The geographical boundaries have been dissolved, the stakeholders' access has increased and convenient channels of distribution of information have been established.

- Richness of Information: It is another element brought by the new media through the variety of genres which if well integrated within the enabling platforms transmits information in powerful ways.

- High Interactivity: The new media has high interactivity, which denotes exchange of quality information between stakeholders.

- Personalization/Customization: It refers to the ability to offer information tailored to meet the needs of a specific stakeholder group.

Below: A table showing New Media features relative to the technology dimension and programme communication significance.

New Media feature	Technology dimension	Programme Communication significance
Ubiquity	World Wide Web	Online information dissemination
Global reach	The internet	Online information dissemination

Interactivity	Information websites	Exchange of information
Information density	The Websites	Using various formats to disseminate programme communication
Richness of Information	Customized websites/tools	Creating organisation/ programme specific website, with either controlled or open access by stakeholders
Social technology	Social websites	Stakeholders Relationships building

The new media has deprived programme managers the monopoly to develop projects. Stakeholders can participate in designing the programme by commenting on specific issues that the programme should address in its short, medium and long term plans or providing feedback on its specific components. Simply put, interactive programme communication is a dialogue between both sides, each actively paying attention to the other. This style of communication has become quite essential in today's digital world given that stakeholders are more advanced in digital technology compared to the past.

How do programme communication specialists know which kind of stakeholder to reach out to or who have been accessing the programme information? The new media technology has provided several options. Among the options is Clickstream analysis (Ralph and George 2013). Clickstream is a recent invention that detects signals generated by each page request. It shows visitors' real-time activity during which each visitor is represented by an icon. The full Clickstream of visitors is viewed after clicking the icon in each category. Also visible is the complete visitors profile and all pages that the visitor viewed in the most recent entry. Data analysis is done and the requests are graphically presented. Webmasters get details of the nature of visitors visiting their websites and use this information to analyse the location and behaviour of the site visitors.

This feature enables tracking stakeholders who may be reached through the new media or have accessed the programme new media platform within a specified period of time. Consequently, sampling of these stakeholders and sourcing their feedback on the programme is made possible, and this can be useful in measuring the impact of the programme on the stakeholders

What are the Factors to Consider When Developing New Media Platforms for programme Communication?

Voice of the stakeholders: The programme team should keenly listen to what stakeholders are saying. Personal bias towards an idea or a proposition may irritate stakeholders who may use the same media to launch a campaign against the same programme. Responding to what stakeholders say is a way of providing more information to them; access to information is a basic human right in the universal declaration of human rights. The stakeholders further transmit the information to their network of stakeholders.

Accept and respond to criticism: In a media that departs from the traditional one-way mass media, relationship-building through dialogue is a strong tool to persuade stakeholders. How the programme manager and the entire programme team respond to criticism and comments from critics matters, or from the beneficiaries determines how successful or not the programme will be. Rudeness harms the programme image and may cause withdrawal of stakeholders support. Calmness and diligence in response promotes the image and create mutually benefitting relationships.

Regular update of information in the platforms: Stakeholders like to see something new every time they access the new media platforms. Regular updates increase the amount of information that stakeholder access; to contribute to the success of the programme.

Facts about actionable data/information: Lying about the important data is disastrous. Unlike the one-way media where the stakeholders would not get an opportunity to respond to misinformation, new media give instantaneous responses and therefore irreparable damage can be caused by dissatisfaction of stakeholders by the accuracy of data/information communicated.

Advantages of using New Media for Programme Communication

• Stakeholders who cannot easily be reached through other channels due to technical limitations can be easily reached through the new media. For example; if a stakeholder is in a location without telephone networks but can access the internet, communication can be carried out through the various new media platforms.

- The programme can harness the knowledge of the both internal and external stakeholders, as they seek responses on various issues through the new media networks. For example; online surveys are good for gathering both quantitative and qualitative data from stakeholders.

- Unlike traditional one way mass communication, the new media allow organizations to get feedback about particular programmes and thus act as platform for measurement of the level of stakeholders support to the programme.

- Programmes targeting the mass audience but lacking financial capability to engage in traditional mass media can benefit from the new media. Networking through new media offers a rewarding opportunity because there is comparatively low cost involved.

- Challenges of using the new media in programme communication

- When the programme team cannot put down ideas in a clear, easy to comprehend manner, stakeholders may be de-motivated to visit their sites.

- Many internal stakeholders who have much to write to promote the programme image are often too busy to write on the new media platforms. Some of those who have time to write know little to write about.

- Using the new media for programme communication requires coherence of strategy, professionalism, commitment, and clearly set goals. Some programmes lack experts to create the needed coherence. Due to this, some new media sites remain un-updated for a long time, driving away the stakeholders.

PROGRESS MONITORING AND RESULTS EVALUATION

Developing a good programme communication strategy does not translate easily to results. It requires progressive monitoring and evaluating of achieve- ments against the set goal, mainly by assessing the degree of achievement of the set performance indicators. For this to happen, the Programme Manager should have a clear technical understanding of which processes within each critical step precede the other and how the success or failure of each step influence the proceeding step and the overall implementation of the pro- gramme communication strategy. This is because timing of some processes is depended on successful completion of the preceding, and therefore a delay of a critical step leads to delay of the subsequent steps. A delay or failure of some critical steps negatively affects strategic initiatives' likelihood of achieving the planned objectives within the planned time and costs. For example, extension of the period for completing key initiatives often leads to higher cost due to additional expenses in man-hours, bills, cost of equipment and other operational compensations. Aligning of communication processes with the strategic initiatives and execution within the critical steps mitigates these unwarranted expenses.

Progress monitoring and results evaluation helps in early identification of the risks that face the communication strategy and may have subsequent impact on the programme strategic goal. Lessons learned in this process should be used in modifying the implementation modality of the strategy to ensure maximum impact.

In general some of the common characteristics of success in using programme communication channels include the following;

- *Grouping stakeholders:* This is one of the markers of success in pro- gramme communication with stakeholders; monitoring involves identifying grouping patterns - either by functionalities within the programme management structure for internal stakeholders or by the interests particularly for the external stakeholders. For example, stakeholders may be grouped by sectors (Finance, Programme, Administration, Security etc), or whether internal (senior management, other) or external (donors, local authorities, other agencies etc).

- *Relevance of the communication*: This was identified as one of the characteristics of results based programme communication in part 2, and revolves around creating easy and edifying communication, anticipation of the stakeholders' information needs and providing well articulated and relevant information to each group of stakeholders. Maintaining relevance requires proactive communication with clear objective of building mutually benefiting relationships. The human dimension discussed earlier during the roll out stage should be critically observed.

- *Regular feedback*: Since the new media and other forms of traditional media such as face-to-face or group meetings provides a two way communication, regular feedback stands out as the strongest indicator of communication success. The nature of feedback should be helpful in weighing whether the stakeholders are happy with the way communication is done or the way the programme is run as a whole. Lack of feedback is a cause for rethinking of the strategy.

- *Establishing a sense of community*: Programme communication should be geared towards making each stakeholder feel like a shareholder in the programme; it should aim at making them feel as they are an important component of the programme, just as an individual is a member of a community, and therefore the success of the programme is their success.

Rolling out a communication strategy is a process with specific milestones as indicated in the strategic spectrum discussed earlier. These can be progressively measured by performance indicators. At times the developed strategy or some options may backfire during the roll out process, which may necessitate a significant change in the identified options. Similarly, midterm evaluation findings may reveal a range of issues that may prompt a decision to change the project communication strategy:

- A need to revamp the flow of information both internally and externally.

- Evidence of gaps that if not filled may hinder effective achievement of the set communication objectives.

- Interest of the stakeholders to modify the communication approaches. The stakeholders may suggest alternative and more convenient strategies.

- Difficulties in getting message across to stakeholders and therefore require dynamic ways of communicating.

- Changes in the timeframe of the project.

- Emergence of new communication tools, such as the use of new media or adoption of new media while the project is underway.

- Expansion of the stakeholders range - new stakeholders come in place, with new information needs i.e. language difference, levels of literacy, conversance with use of communication technology etc.

Conclusion

The essence of communication is not just to pass the message across, but also to make the desired impact. Programme communication is obviously the manifestation of the technical aspect of communication that goes beyond the pure act of information exchange, to a strategic initiative at the core of all programming processes. While multiple approaches may be adopted to initiate and implement a programme communication strategy, the underlying factor is that the stakeholders whether internal or external hold the tools for measurement of the relevance of communication: - if whatever is communicated effectively meets their information and communication needs (Relevance). This is one key performance metric. It is on the basis on this metric that feedback is provided and the process continues within the circularity of communication processes. Efficiency is evaluated against the strategy and its implementation, how it responds to the programmatic processes and propels the programme within the expectations of the stakeholders. A well designed and executed communication strategy reduces the risks of omitting important stakeholders (inclusiveness) in communication while at the same time ensuring that all that is communicated is not done by chance (Predictability); that there is a well laid down plan that can transcend personalities and with-stand competing values and stakeholders' contexts related risks.

BIBLIOGRAPHY

Alexandrova, Ekaterina. Using New Media Effectivelly: An analysis of Barack Obama's election Campeign aimed at Young Americans: Masters Thesis; New York; Fordham University, 2010.

Burstain, David. Innovation Agents: Oscar Morales and One Million Voices Against FARC. Fast Company 2012. Retrieved Jan 2015 from www.fastcompany.com.

Cameron, Kim & Quinn, Robert. Competing Values Leadership. Edward Elgar Publishing, 2006.

Chuck, Martin. Tough Management: Corporate Truth verses Street Truth. McGrow Hill Professional, 2005.

Department of Defence, United States of America: Principles of Strategic Communication, 2008.

FTI Consulting. Strategic Initiatives Study: Adapting Corporate Strategy to the Changing Economy. Author, 2010.

Google (2014). Retrieved from www.google.co.ke/?gwsrd=ssl#q=Communication.

Guffey, M & Loewy D,. Essentials of Busines Communication. South Western Cengage Learning, 2010.

Independent Consulting Bootcamp. Difference between a Project and a Programme. Author. 2005. Retrieved www. Independent-consulting-bootcamp.com.

Immanuel Kant. Critique of Pure Reason, trans. Norman Kemp Smith. New York: St Martin's Press 1965.

Project Management Institute. The High Cost of Low Performance: The Essential Role of Communications. Author, 2013.

Project Management Institute (2014) Pulse of the Profession. Retrieved 6 January 2015, from http://www.pmi.org/learning/pulse.aspx.

Kristen Wolf. Now Hear This; The Nine Laws of Successful Advocacy Communications. Washington DC. Fenton Communications.,2001.

Quinn, Robert. Diagnosing and changing organizational culture: based on the competing value. John Willey and Sons, 2005.

Richard Wike and Russ Oates. Emerging Nations Embrace Internet, Mobile Technology, Cell Phones Nearly Ubiquitous in Many Countries. PewResearch Centre, 2013.

Saussure, F.de. Course in General Linguistics (trans.Roy Harris). london: Duckworth, 1983.

Shehu, Z & Akintoye, A,. The Critical Success Factors for Effective Programme Management: A pragmatic Approach. The Build & Human environmental Review. Volume 2, 2009. Retrieved 9 January 2019 from www.tbher.org/index.php/tbher/article/viewFile/9/9

Shing, LI KA. Technology as our Enabler. Li Ka Shing Foundation, 2005.

Straubhaar, Joseph. Media Now: Understanding Media, Culture, and Technology. Cengage Learning, 2008.

Towers Watson. How the Fundamentals Have Evolved and the Best Adapt: 2013-2014 Change and Communication ROI Study: The 10th Anniversary Report, 2014.

Turner, Geoff. Proceedings of the 3rd European Conference on Intellectual Capital. Academic Conferences Limited, 2011.

The Strategic Communications Division of FTI Consulting. Strategic Initiatives Study: Adapting Corporate Strategy to the Changing

Economy. Author, 2010.

UN OCHA. Humanitarianism in the Network Age; OCHA Policy and Studies Series. United Nations Publication, 2012.

Stratcomexperts is committed to excellence
in programme communication. Our team of highly trained and experienced
professionals, consultants and volunteers
work together to offer the most appropriate advice and support to our clients on
short and longer term basis.

Stratcomeexperts reflect in every aspect the belief
advocated by the founders

that

*'advancing strategic programme communication as a critical success factor is in itself an
evidence of results driven programming '*

If you would like further information

contact us on:
+254725740024

or send an email:
info@stratcomexperts.com
www.stratcomexperts.com

Stratcom Experts
P.O. Box 9220 – 00300
Nairobi, Kenya

STRATCOM EXPERTS
COMMUNICATION SOLUTIONS

www.ingramcontent.com/pod-product-compliance
Lightning Source LLC
Chambersburg PA
CBHW070832180526
45168CB00002B/813